MW00477067

EQUALITY LOST
Essays in Torah Commentary, Halacha, and Jewish Thought

EQUALITY LOST

Essays in Torah Commentary, Halacha, and Jewish Thought

Rabbi Yehuda Henkin

Urim Publications
Jerusalem
1999 / 5759

Equality Lost: Essays in Torah Commentary, Halacha, and
Jewish Thought
© Urim Publications and Lambda Publishers, Inc.
Urim Publications, P.O.Box 52287 Jerusalem 91521 Israel
First Edition

Distributed by:

Lambda Publishers, Inc.
3709 13th Avenue
Brooklyn, New York 11218 U.S.A.
Tel: 718-972-5449 Fax: 718-972-6307
mh@ejudaica.com

ISBN 965-7108-01-2

CONTENTS

4 Contents

Jewish Thought

Biography

FOREWORD

This book focuses on a number of different areas of Jewish interest.

Torah Commentary: One of the marks of a simple interpretation (*peshat*) is that once made, it seems obvious, even if no one had thought of it before.

The writing of new *peshat* on the narrative sections of the Torah is famously associated with the *Rashbam* (13th century France), but in fact is engaged in by all the major commentators: *Rashi*, *Ibn Ezra*, *Ramban*, *Sforno* and others. This is true even when the interpretations go against the Talmud and Midrash. *Or haChaim* writes in the introduction to his commentary on the Torah: "Sometimes I will exercise the writer's quill in simple explanations of Scripture in a way different from what *chaza"l* expounded. I have made clear I do not dispute in the slightest those who came first, but permission has been granted to [independently] till and sow [the Torah]." Similarly, at the beginning of his commentary to *Ha'azinu*: "Even though those who preceded us chose a different path, we have already noted that there are seventy faces to the Torah. In matters of *aggadah* our interpretations may even contradict theirs, as long as the contradiction is not in matters of Halacha."

In 1971, I asked my sainted grandfather, Rabbi Yosef Eliyahu Henkin זצ״ל, whether it was permissible to interpret non-halachic parts of the Torah in ways different from those of *chaza"l*. He answered, "Yes, provided the intention is to strengthen *yirat shamayim*."

Halacha: I have often been asked to translate my responsa into English, but I have felt that a public unfamiliar with *teshuvot* in Hebrew should probably not be reading them in translation, given the disputatious and highly technical nature of the genre. On the other hand, most of the halachic articles in this book were written in response to what I perceived to be erroneous presentations of Halacha in English, which demanded a reply. Such presentations can stand alone and unchallenged for years if not decades. Although the secular academic level of the Orthodox English-reading public is very high, most readers are poorly educated in rabbinic texts and unable to critically evaluate what they read.

Halachic literary tradition places a premium on caution and on deference to authority; Western and particularly academic mores, in contrast, stress boldness and innovation. Today, encyclopedias, computers, and other means of accessing information simplify halachic research; the old rule-of-thumb "unless you know a lot about everything, you know little about anything" ostensibly no longer applies. The result has been a diminution of the expertise once demanded for entry into the field of Halacha. This has been particularly felt in the United States with the passing of accepted halachic arbiters such as R. Henkin, R. Feinstein, and R. Soloveitchik, *z"l*.

Jewish Thought: To understand G-d's hand in history I have employed inductive reasoning and extrapolated from events as best I can. The reason is that, as opposed to Halacha which, having been given at Sinai, is *lo bashamayim* (not in heaven), G-d's reasons and considerations are very much *bashamayim* and not open to *a priori* deduction. Scripture, however, can provide precedents, and rabbinical exegesis, the means to analyze them.

Biography: The memory of my grandfather *z"l* is revered by tens of thousands, but a generation is reaching maturity which "knew not Yosef" while even his contemporaries knew few details of his life in Europe. This is the first serious biographical account to appear in English.

A religion can be evaluated either by reference to its typical practitioners or by the ideal-types it produces; my grandfather was an example of an ideal-type of Judaism. Jews with his combination of piety, honesty, and humility (leaving his prodigious learning aside, for the moment) exist even now; on the other hand, there are deprived communities today whose children grow up without ever having met such a *tzaddik*.

* * *

Many if not all of the issues in this book have been discussed in my previous books in Hebrew, consisting of three volumes of halachic responsa *Bnei Banim*, a commentary on the narrative parts of the Torah *Chibah Yeteirah*, a monograph on contemporary events *Perakim beHavanat Me'ora'ot Zemaneinu*, and a collection of essays *Tavevan uKeshot* ("Acts of Kindness and Truth").

There is much more material there than here, and it is my hope that readers able to understand Hebrew will be motivated to look for them. (Available through Lambda Publishers in New York or from me at P.O.Box 35173, Jerusalem.)

I acknowledge with thanks those periodicals which published articles subsequently adapted as chapters in this book: the *Jewish Bible Quarterly* (chapter 2), *The Jewish Press* (chapter 14) and the *Jewish Observer* (chapter 15). I should also mention periodicals that did not: *Tradition* magazine which rejected, over time, articles that appear here as chapters 2, 11, and 13(!), and the *Journal of Halacha and Contemporary Society* which declined articles that appear as chapters 8, 10, and 11. I leave it to the reader to draw his or her own conclusions.

My gratitude to Urim Publications and Lambda Publishers for their vision and encouragement, and to my publisher Tzvi Mauer and to Gloria Kanefsky for their comments.

Finally, my love, thanks, and gratitude to my wife, *Rabbanit* Chana. I would expand on this, if not for her objections to thanking her in public.

Yehuda Herzl Henkin
Jerusalem
Tevet 5759

My father, Dr. Avraham Hillel Henkin *z"l*, died in his apartment near ours in Jerusalem on 9 *Sivan* 5758, aged 86. He was a distinguished Jewish educator, for many years director of the Bureau of Jewish Education in New Haven, and subsequently dean of Herzliah Hebrew Teachers College in New York, and a past president of the National Council of Jewish Education. He was completely devoted to his family and community. He was the most honest of men; I never heard a falsehood cross his lips. ‫ת.נ.צ.ב.ה‬.

Y. H. H.

TORAH COMMENTARY

Chapter One

EQUALITY LOST:
THE SECOND CHAPTER OF *BEREISHIT*

We find a number of surprises in the creation of woman in chapter two of *Bereishit*. The first surprise is that the creation occurs even though male and female have already been created in chapter one. Even a slight examination, however, reveals that the two accounts are complementary: the first chapter deals with man's physical nature, while the second charts his character and interpersonal relationships. These relationships are unique to mankind, in contrast to "Be fruitful and multiply" in chapter one which applies equally to other species, and even in contrast to "and rule over the fish of the sea and the birds of the sky and all the beasts" which places man at the head of the food chain yet does not distinguish his essence from that of other creatures. Chapter one deals with *male and female* and chapter two with *man and woman*; they are not the same.

We will focus, therefore, on a different surprise, the remarkable timing of the creation of woman in chapter two. G-d did not, as we might have expected, create man and woman at the same time, nor even the one immediately after the other. Instead, G-d (a) created Adam and (b) placed him in the Garden of Eden. Next, He (c) commanded him "but from the tree of knowledge of Good and Evil—do not eat from it..." Only then did He

(d) declare "It is not good for man to be alone," (e) parade the animals before man and, finally, (f) create Eve.

The conclusion is inescapable: woman was created *in response* to the giving of the commandment not to eat from the tree. Apart from being clearly indicated by the juxtaposition of events, this also makes perfect sense, for otherwise in what way was it "not good" for man in the Garden of Eden? Man lacked nothing in the garden, which is, as is known, a synonym for paradise. No cloud darkened his sky—until he was commanded not to eat from the tree. Then and only then was he confronted with the challenge of overcoming his curiosity or carelessness; his *yeitzer hara*, if you will. G-d provided a companion to assist him in observing the *mitzvah*, a theme also found in rabbinic literature.[1]

Support for this interpretation can be brought from use of the phrase "It is not good" (*lo tov*) elsewhere in Scripture. Yitro's protest to Moshe "*lo tov hadavar asher atah oseh*" ("What you are doing is not good" *Shemot* 18:17), does not question the latter's good intentions or merit; it means that Moshe will fail in his misguided attempt to judge the people alone. Similarly, David's "*lo tov hadavar hazeh asher asita*" (I Samuel 26:16) criticizes Avner's ineptitude in guarding Sha'ul. Thus, in the garden, G-d said *lo tov heyot ha'adam levado*, which is to say: giving the commandment to man to observe while he is all alone is not a good idea; it *won't work.*

Woman helped man violate the commandment rather than observe it: yet another surprise. Did G-d make a *mistake?* Here the reader may counter that, within the parameters of the Creation narrative, G-d indeed made "mistakes." Did He not create man and then regret His handiwork, "*ki nichamti ki asitim*" (*Bereishit* 6:7)? However, there is a fundamental difference between G-d's words before the Flood and his statement in chapter two. The creation of man in chapter one was not accompanied by qualitative evaluation; the daily summation "and G-d saw that it was good" is conspicuously absent. Leaving aside the age-old problem of reconciling man's free-will with G-d's omniscience and foreknowledge, we may say that G-d created humanity as an experiment and let man determine the results; the fact that the experiment almost failed reflects no error on His part. Not so with the creation of woman in chapter two. "It is not good for man to be alone..." is a categorical statement of fact. It is theologically *impossible* for such a declaration to be erroneous; how, then, are we to comprehend Eve's leading Adam into sin?

The problem is more apparent than real. G-d did not say it is good for man to have a mate, only that it is *not good* for him *not* to have one. Marriages are not guaranteed success. "*Matza*" or "*motzei*," goes the ancient question: is it "He who has found (*matza*) a wife, has found good" (Proverbs 18:22) or perhaps "I find (*motzei*) the woman to be more bitter than death" (Ecclesiastes 7:26)?[2] Judaism recognizes the reality of divorce, and certainly there are unhappy and unsuccessful marriages even when, for various reasons, divorce is not considered. Yet the Rabbis are unequivocal, "One should not be without a wife..."[3] Here, too, G-d made no claims as to the outcome of giving man a wife, only that there was no alternative. Together, man and woman might succeed in following His Word or they might fail; alone, man's failure was inevitable.

We can now understand the second half of G-d's declaration in chapter two: *"e'eseh lo eizer kenegdo,"* usually translated as "I will make him a help meet [=suitable] for him" or, midrashically, "opposed to him." The form *keneged* with a *kaf* is found nowhere else in Scripture, and we must therefore rely on Talmudic parallels. The simplest meaning is undoubtedly "equal to him," as in *"talmud Torah keneged kulam,"* "the study of Torah is equal to them all"[4] and many similar statements.

G-d created woman equal to man in order to assist him in fulfilling the commandment, and the reason is clear: to truly influence man for good or for ill, his helper had to rival him in intellect and comprehension. Thus, in chapter two, "G-d formed...all the beasts of the field and all the birds of heaven and brought them to man...and did not find him an *eizer kenegdo,*" because man is not swayed by an inferior being. A horse or a dog can provide companionship, but cannot prevail upon man to observe G-d's Word. Only woman, woven from the same cloth as was man, "bone of my bones and flesh of my flesh," was equal to him and equal to the task.

What remains to be explained is what went wrong. Our interpretation is that the *zilzul*—disrespect, belittlement, underestimation—by one party of the other in spite of their having been created equal, led to the violation of the commandment with its tragic results for mankind. Before explicating Adam's attitude to his wife in the garden of Eden, however, we will note three other cases of *zilzul* and its consequences in the book of *Bereishit.*

Noah left the ark and, we are told in chapter 9, he drank himself into stupefaction and "uncovered himself in his tent. Ham, father of Canaan, saw his father's nakedness and told his two brothers outside." In response, Noah later cursed Ham's progeny. We are not told what exactly Ham did to his drunken father to merit such a curse; one interpretation, in Gemara *Sanhedrin* (70a), is that he committed a homosexual act. But even if all Ham did was to coolly note his father's nakedness and invite his brothers to join in viewing the spectacle, it certainly was a shocking display of filial irreverence on his part, and the question arises: what led Ham to behave in such a fashion?

We can ascertain an answer by noting a superfluity in the introductory verse of the Masoretic *parshah* which contains the affair: "The sons of Noah, those leaving the ark, were Shem, Ham and Yafet." We already know that they had all been in the ark, and so what does "those leaving the ark" come to tell us? In all likelihood, it establishes a link between leaving the ark in chapter 8 and the episode of Noah and Ham in chapter 9, and inspection indeed reveals such a link. G-d had told Noah, "Leave the ark, you and your wife and your sons and their wives with you," listing Noah's wife before his sons. Noah, however, did the opposite: "Noah and his sons and his wife and his sons' wives left the ark." He advanced his sons before his wife. Children copy their parents' behavior: Noah displayed *zilzul* of his wife and consequently Ham displayed *zilzul* of his father.

A virtually identical episode can be found in chapter 19. After the destruction of Sodom, Lot and his two daughters took refuge in a cave, "and they made their father drink wine that night. The older daughter came and slept with her father." The next night they made Lot drunk again, and this time the younger daughter slept

with her father. The account concludes with the statement that "Lot's two daughters (*shtei banot*) became
pregnant from their father." In context, the number two
of "two daughters" seems completely redundant, and
there is little doubt that it comes to remind us of Lot's
words in offering his daughters to the mob earlier in the
chapter, "Here, now, I have two daughters (*shtei
banot*)..." Lot displayed *zilzul* of his daughters and they
responded in kind.

Yet another example of the pernicious and
far-reaching effects of disrespect can be found in the
chain of events in chapter 35 of *Bereishit*. Yaakov had
settled in Shechem, upon his return from Padan Aram,
and when forced to leave Shechem he traveled to Bet El,
and from there to Efrat and then to beyond Migdal Eider.
Where he did *not* go was to Hebron to visit his aged
father, and the reasons for this seeming lack of filial
respect are obscure. In any case, the consequences were
not long in coming: "It happened, when Israel dwelled in
that land, that Reuven went and lay with his father's
concubine, Bilha. And Israel heard." The Rabbis explain
that Reuven merely moved Bilha's bed from one tent to
another,[5] but even such interference in the sleeping
arrangements of his father represented a gross lack of
respect. The connection seems clear: Yaakov failed to
honor his own father, or at least Reuven perceived him
as not doing so, and so Reuven failed to honor him. The
narrative continues with a sudden enumeration of
Yaakov's children: "The sons of Yaakov were twelve..."
What has this to do with what came before? Our interpretation is that the point being made is that Reuven was
just the beginning: Yaakov had another eleven sons, and
if he persisted in not honoring his father the others

would follow in Reuven's footsteps. Yaakov fully realized the danger of this happening and so, immediately after the listing of his sons, "Yaakov came to [visit] his father Yitzchak, to Mamre, Kiryat Arba..."

Zilzul, then, is operative in a number of episodes in *Bereishit*, and in fact its roots stretch back to the garden of Eden. G-d said to man prior to creating woman, "...but from the tree of knowledge of Good and Evil—do not eat from it, for you will die on the day you eat from it." Woman, however, told the serpent "...but from the fruit of the tree which is in the midst of the garden, G-d said, 'Don't eat from it and don't touch it, lest you die.'" The Rabbis disagree as to the source of "and don't touch it." According to *Bereishit Rabbah*, (15:3) woman added it herself, while according to *Avot deRabi Natan* (1:5) man added it when he conveyed the warning to his wife. If we accept the traditional explanation that woman first touched the fruit, noted that she was still alive and concluded erroneously that she could also eat from it without being punished,[6] we must adopt *Avot deRabi Natan*'s version, for if she herself added "and don't touch it" she could hardly have confused her own words with G-d's.

Whether or not Adam treated Eve with contempt by inflating G-d's prohibition to include touching—as if she couldn't be relied upon to observe the commandment as given—his attitude to her is clear from what he did *not* tell her. Woman said, "the tree which is in the midst of the garden." Why didn't she call it by name, the tree of knowledge of good and evil? Moreover, the serpent said, "the day you eat from it your eyes will be opened and you will be like gods, knowers of good and evil." Since the tree's *name* was "tree of knowledge of good and evil," what did the serpent tell woman that she didn't already know?

Woman didn't know the name of the tree. She didn't know, because man didn't tell her. He treated her like a child, telling her what to do without sharing with her the information he himself received from G-d. The serpent gained her confidence by revealing that which her husband had withheld from her, and mixed truth with the fateful untruth, "You will not die..."

Man and woman were created equal, but from the first he related to her as an inferior; by doing so he caused *her* to stumble and the result was that she caused *him* to stumble, measure for measure. We still suffer the consequences of this primordial *zilzul*, in the form of the respective curses given man and woman.

This is not advocacy of radical egalitarianism. The Torah prescribes different roles for men and women, and not everything "natural" is desirable or beneficial. The exigencies of society and civilization are different from those in the garden of Eden. Indeed, one of the points of the second and third chapters of *Bereishit* is to explain just how man and woman, although created equal, came to be unequal. But "by the sweat of your brow you shall eat bread" is a curse and not a commandment, and man is permitted to automate the growing of food; "in pain you shall bear children" does not rule out the use of anesthesia in childbirth; and so, too, "your craving will be for your husband, and he will rule over you" is descriptive and not prescriptive. The absence of *zilzul* between spouses, the recognition of the equal capabilities of man and woman, is a step towards fulfilling G-d's intention that the one strengthen the other in observance of His Word.

Notes

1. See Babylonian Talmud (BT), *Shabbat* 12a.

2. BT *Yevamot* 63b.

3. *Ibid.*, 61b.

4. Mishna, *Peah* 1:1.

5. BT *Shabbat* 55b.

6. *Bereishit Rabbah* itself brings this explanation, and see *Matnot Kehunah*, *ad loc.*

Chapter Two

PESHAT AS AN INNOVATIVE METHOD IN TORAH COMMENTARY

We usually view *peshat* (the simple interpretation of the text) as being severely limited vis-a-vis *derash* (the aggadic or homiletical interpretation). The master of *peshat* is constrained by the language and parameters of the story, while the master of *derash* is free to connect seemingly unrelated episodes, to develop original themes, to provide details whenever the text is silent, and, in general, to embellish Scripture as best G-d inspires him or her.

Certainly, there are dull and unimaginative works that claim to be *peshat*. We find no lack of modern commentaries replete with sterile philological analyses, with background descriptions which add little to our understanding of the text and nothing to our religious sensibilities, and with unpersuasive and unsatisfying interpretations of various kinds.

This description, however, does injustice to the employment of *peshat*, at least in the narrative sections of the Torah. The power of *peshat* lies precisely in that it deals with the "truth" of the narrative. It seeks to determine what actually happened. Had we been there, this is what we would have seen! To accomplish this the master of *peshat* needs a generous measure of imagination and intuition, as well as a finely-developed detective sense and a sensitivity to nuances in language. In the Torah, the cryptic and the elliptic are more prevalent than the explicit.[1] And, even when details are provided, we still don't know why the protagonists behaved in one way and not in another.

What, then, divides *peshat* from *derash* in this regard? The master of *peshat* must rely on his "knowledge of people's behavior" (*beki'uto bederech eretz shel bnei adam*), to quote *Rashbam* on *Vayikra* 13:2. He is bound by reality as he understands it. But this restriction is, in fact, the source of his strength.

Let me give four examples from my Hebrew commentary on the Torah, *Chibah Yeteirah: Chiddushim bePeshat haTorah.*

The Tower of Bavel

> *HaShem* (G-d) went down to see the city and the tower which men built. *HaShem* said, "They are truly one people and have one language (*safah*).This has enabled them to start, and now nothing they plan on doing will be beyond them. Let us go down and confuse their language (*sefatam*) so that one will not understand the language (*sefat*) of his fellow." From there *haShem* scattered them all over the land, and they stopped building the city. (*Bereishit* 11:5–8)

This account seems hardly susceptible to explanation on the basis of "knowledge of people's behavior." How can we explain circumstances in which inhabitants wake up one morning and discover that they cannot understand each other? That they speak foreign languages?

Even if what took place was miraculous, moreover, it is unclear what exactly happened. Who did not understand whom? Husbands their wives, or relatives other family members? Or perhaps all members of a family continued to talk to each other, but not to members of other families? How many languages were created—if there were 2,000 families, did they speak 2,000 languages? And why didn't they attempt to learn a common language all over again?

We may, however, offer a different explanation. The Torah here is very precise in its use of the Hebrew terms for "speech" or "language." Regarding the descendants of Noah becoming nations in chapter 10 of *Bereishit*, the term *lashon* is used three times ("*lileshono*," "*lileshonotam*," "*lileshonotam*"), but regarding Bavel in chapter 11 the term *safah* is used five times ("*safah*," "*safah*," "*sefatam*," "*sefat*," "*sefat*"). It is clear that *lashon* and *safah* are not the same.

Lashon is not used in the story of the Tower of Bavel, for G-d did not mix up their *lashon* but rather their *safah*. According to an opinion in the Jerusalem Talmud,[2] they all understood 70 languages in any case. Rather, *safah* means opinion, as in Zephania (13:9), "I will bring the nations to a clear opinion (*safah berurah*) to call on the name of *haShem*" (and see *Radak* there). In Bavel, they were all of the same mind. As the midrash states: they all loved each other.[3] Therefore, "This has enabled them to start, and now nothing they plan on doing will be beyond them." Even G-d would not be able to control them, as it were, as the Sages expounded from Hosea (4:17), "If Efraim is united, [even] in idol-worship—leave him alone."[4] Therefore the Lord mixed up *sefatam*, meaning, He sowed dissension among them.

The scene has now been completely transformed. The episode of the tower of Bavel enters the domain of *peshat*. Far from being a miraculous episode and remote from our own experience, it emerges as a historical event easy to imagine. And above all, the commentary is solidly based on the Torah itself: highlighted by the different usages of "*lashon*" and "*safah*."

Avraham's Oath

> The king of Sodom said to Avram: "Give me the people and keep the property for yourself." Avram replied to the king of Sodom: "I have raised my hand to *haShem*, the supreme G-d, owner of heaven and earth. From a string to a shoe-lace I will take nothing of yours, lest you say, 'I made Avram rich.'" (*Bereishit* 14:21–23)

The problem with Avraham's statement is that he says none of the things the commentators attribute to him. *Rashi* explained his argument as being that he had no need for goods, since G-d had promised to enrich him. *Ramban* wrote that Avraham intended to make the property sacred and set aside for G-d. *Or haChaim* commented that he did not wish others to say that he was motivated by greed.

The king of Sodom, however, said "keep the property," and Avraham rejected his offer "lest you say, 'I made Avram rich.'" Why was the king of Sodom so ready to give up his wealth? And why would he want to claim, publicly, that he enriched Avraham—what would he gain by saying so? We also need to understand why Avraham would mind if anyone said so. Why did he refuse gifts only from the king of Sodom, but accepted them earlier from Pharaoh and later from Avimelech?

To explain all this, we must note Avraham's emphasis "lest *you* say (*velo tomar*)" and not simply "lest people say" or "lest it be said." The king of Sodom wanted Avraham to be indebted to *him*. The Torah does not say that the four attacking kings were killed, only that Avraham "beat and pursued them" (*Bereishit* 14:15), and perhaps they would return and attack a second time. By publicizing that he enriched Avraham and that, therefore, Avraham owed him a favor, the king of Sodom sought to ensure that Avraham would again come to his rescue. Avraham therefore declined to take anything from him, "lest you say, 'I made Avram rich.'"

Avraham's words, it turns out, are precise and to the point. But we have gained more than merely an attractive explanation. We have uncovered a new facet of Avraham's personality: not just righteous, faithful, pure, and so forth, but also pragmatic and farsighted. One can speculate that were he alive today he would make an excellent Secretary of State.

This, too, is the task of the master of *peshat*: to take the bare bones of the Torah's descriptions of the forefathers and cover them with sinews and flesh, until it seems that we personally knew them.

Rivka and the Camels

> The servant ran to meet her, and said, "Let me have a little water from your pitcher." She said, "Drink, sir," and hurried and took her pitcher in her hands and let him drink. She finished letting him drink, and said, "I will also draw water for your camels, until they finish drinking." She hurried and emptied her pitcher into the trough, and again ran to the well to draw water and drew for all his camels. (*Bereishit* 24:17–20)

Eliezer (the traditional identification of the servant) came with 10 camels, capable of drinking altogether 140 gallons of water when they came from the desert. Indeed, there are those who have waxed poetic over Rivka's display of devotion in filling and emptying her pitcher hundreds of times to let them drink their fill!

But such a description is not credible. First, how does a young girl have the physical strength for such a task? Second, what kind of test was this for Rivka—was Eliezer looking for a slave-girl for Isaac? And was it not a profanation of the Name of G-d to let her labor to such an extent without lifting a finger to help her?

Rather, Eliezer had been careful in his choice of words. He had stipulated: "And she will say, 'Drink (*shteh*),'" meaning, he should drink from her pitcher, "...and I will also water (*ashkeh*) your camels" (24:14), not from the pitcher, but as in *Devarim* 11:10, "you irrigated (*hishkita*) [the fields in Egypt] with your feet." In Egypt the fields were watered by use of water-wheels and other machines which were turned by pedals or by pushing. Here, too, a girl could draw water for the camels relatively easily by machine, and not with her pitcher. Haran was a large city on a traveled route and many caravans came there, not to mention the city's own cattle, and they most probably had machinery for drawing water for them as was customary in those days. This is the meaning of "she...emptied her pitcher into the trough." After the men finished drinking, she emptied the water which was left in her pitcher into the trough, "and again ran to the well to draw [water] and drew for all his camels," using the water-wheel.

Should one feel that this *peshat* detracts from Rivka's greatness, the Torah has a different way to stress her special qualities. Rivka established her credentials (*chazakah*) by displaying alacrity three times in acts of kindness:[5] "She *hurried* and took her pitcher in her hands and let him drink... She *hurried* and emptied her pitcher into the trough...and again *ran* to the well to draw water" (24:18, 20). Avraham had similarly hastened to do acts of kindness: "He *ran* to meet them from the door of the tent... Avraham *hurried* to the tent...Avraham *ran* to the cattle" (15:2, 6–7). That is why Rivka merited being his daughter-in-law.

"When War Calls"

> He [the king of Egypt] said to his people: "The Israelite people is now numerous, and too strong for us. Let us deal wisely with it [the Israelite people] lest it grow, for when war comes (*tikrenah*) it, too, will join our enemies and fight us, and leave the country." (*Shemot* 1:9–10)

The problem is well-known. What did the Egyptian empire fear, and why? To answer this we should note that "*tikrenah*," from the root *kuf resh aleph*, can mean befall or occur,[6] but it can also mean "call": that is to say, war will call the Egyptians. The Egyptian army never waited for its enemies to invade Egypt, but marched out to Canaan or Syria or Libya to do battle, as in the war with King Yoshiya (II Chronicles 35). Therefore, Pharaoh "said to his people"—the people who would be left behind when the army was called to war. Egypt had no fear when its army was at home, but "when war calls" and the army marched out to fight, the Israelites "will join our enemies and fight us, and leave the country," before the army returned to crush the rebellion.

Pharaoh's seemingly exaggerated fears were in fact realistic. One can easily imagine the mood in Egypt when he spoke to his people.

Without need for further examples, one may sum up the special challenges and accomplishments of the master of *peshat*. If he does his work well, invests imagination and insight, and merits assistance from Heaven, he may find himself moved and electrified by his discoveries, no less than is an archeologist who uncovers artifacts from a distant time. The master of *peshat* walks in the footsteps of the forefathers and ponders their words and actions, until it seems to him that he has stood in their presence. He uncovers facts and details which have been hidden for thousands of years.

The gates of *peshat* are never closed. Each generation discovers *peshat* according to its understanding and experience in life. The master of *peshat*, like his colleague the master of *derash*, finds in the Torah an inexhaustible source of inspiration and discovery.

Notes

1. For an arresting contrast of Biblical terseness with Homeric prolixity, see Eric Auerbach, *Mimesis*, chap. 1.

2. BT *Megillah* 1:9.

3. *Bereishit Rabbah*, 38:6.

4. *Ibid.*

5. This insight is my wife's.

6. See *Bereishit* 49:1; *Vayikra* 10:19.

Chapter Three

DISTINGUISHING *PESHAT* FROM *DERASH*

Torah exegesis is traditionally divided into four categories: *peshat*, *remez*, *derash* and *sod*, forming the acrostic *PaRDeS* (literally: orchard).

Sod (literally: secret) is mystical or esoteric interpretation. Nothing further will be said here about it, other than that *sod* employs unfettered metaphor and pure symbolism to link events and personages to Divine forces and historic processes.

Remez (literally: hint) finds oblique references in the text to events often far removed from its immediate time and place. An example of this can be found in my Torah commentary, *Chibah Yeteirah*: In *Bereishit* 30:1, Rachel told Yaakov, "Give me children (*banim*), or else I die." *Banim* translates as "sons" or "children," in the plural. So, too, when she eventually had a child, "...she called his name Yosef, saying 'May *haShem* afford me *another* [or: a different] son'" (v. 24). Apparently, having only one son was insufficient.

The *remez* is to the fact that Efraim and Menashe, the tribes descended from Yosef, were among the Ten Tribes exiled by Assyria who never returned. If Rachel had had only one son her seed would have been eradicated; her future was secured only through the descendants of her second son, Binyamin.

Derash, aggadic and homiletic exposition, constitutes the main non-legal exegetical activity of the rabbis of the Talmud and Midrash. Contrary to misconception, *derash* usually relies on some textual reading. An example is the *Midrash Rabbah* to *Bereishit* 25:22. On the verse describing Rivka's pregnancy, "the children struggled together within her (*vayitrotzetzu habanim bekirbah*)," the Midrash relates: "When Rivka passed houses of prayer and study, Yaakov struggled to emerge, and when she passed houses of idol worship, Esau ran and struggled to emerge." This has not one but two textual pegs. First, the verb *vayitrotzetzu* contains the root letters *resh tzadi* which form the word *ratz* (to run). Second, in the unvocalized Torah "*bekirbah* (within her [womb])" can just as easily be read *bekarvah* (when she came close). Came close to what? The Midrash follows.

Peshat is the "simple" or "plain" import of the text. The text itself consists of letters, words, sentences, chapters, and larger units. Sometimes the meaning of a word or sentence taken alone differs from its meaning in a wider context. In that case, the latter is almost invariably *peshat* while the former is a source for *derash*.

There can be more than one *peshat* in a given passage. Often, the language leaves ample room for different interpretations. For example, in *Vayikra* 19:17, "You shall not hate your brother in your heart; definitely rebuke your neighbor, and do not bear (*velo tisa alav*) sin about him," the words *tisa alav* can mean at least three different things as seen in other texts of the Bible:

1) In *Vayikra* 22:9, "*velo* **yisu alav** *cheit*" means that "they should not *bear* sin *because of* it [ritual impurity]." Following this usage, the verse in chapter 19 is a warning lest you yourself sin when rebuking your neighbor, e.g., by shaming him publicly.[1]

2) In *Devarim* 25:49, "**Yisa** *haShem* **alecha** *goi mirachok*" means that "G-d will *bring* a nation from afar *upon* you." According to this meaning, our verse warns against rebuking your neighbor if by doing so you bring sin upon *him*, i.e., if thus far he acted out of ignorance, but if rebuked would then sin willfully, this would be a far greater sin.[2]

3) In II Kings 9:25, "**nasa alav** *et hamasa*" means that the prophet "*spoke* G-d's words *about* [the fate of Ahab's family]." The verse in *Vayikra* would thus mean not to attribute sin to your neighbor, that is to say: don't assume he is a willful sinner who can't be changed and that therefore there is no point in talking to him. Don't hate your neighbor in your heart, but instead openly remonstrate with him.

In addition, the text alone is often insufficient to provide any complete picture of what is going on, particularly in the narrative sections of the Torah. The reason for this is the extreme terseness of the Biblical text: the background to the events, the thoughts of the protaganists and other important information are frequently missing and need to be generated. Both *peshat* and *derash* aim to fill these gaps. How can we distinguish between the two types of commentary?

I suggest three criteria for distinguishing between *peshat* and *derash* as well as between various degrees of *peshat*: **necessity**, **economy** and **plausibility**.[3] To illustrate, we may use the midrash concerning Rivka's pregnancy mentioned above, "When Rivka would pass houses of prayer and study..." It fails the three criteria: it is unnecessary, in that to explain the Hebrew "*vayi-trotzetzu habanim bekirbah*" as simply a description of a difficult twin pregnancy leaves no textual difficulty or unanswered question. It lacks economy, in that it introduces new elements, such as houses of prayer and study, which are nowhere indicated in the text. Finally, it lacks plausibility: fetuses do not behave that way, in our experience, and there is no reason to suppose that we are dealing with a miracle.

In fact, the midrash is not talking about Yaakov and Esau, Rivka's children, at all. Talmudic thought rejects the notion that an individual can be an idol-worshipper or a monotheist from his mother's womb.[4] Rather, the political/religious message intended is that the Jewish people from its inception has been God-fearing, while Rome (=Edom=Esau) has been idolatrous.

Notes

1. BT *Archin* 17b. *R. Yonah* in *Shaarei Teshuvah* 3:72 explains the verse as meaning: rebuke your neighbor lest his sin be accounted as yours since you could have prevented it. According to this the verse is a Biblical source for *areivut*, the religious responsibility one has for another. I have suggested that the Talmud does not propose this interpretation because the obligation to rebuke applies even to bad practices such as drunkenness that are not, strictly-speaking, sins; see my *Bnei Banim*, II, no. 26.

2. This is a Biblical source for the Talmudic dictum " *mutav sheyihyu shogegin ve'al yihyu mezidin* (better that they should be ignorant sinners than willful ones)"; see *Bnei Banim*, II, no. 27 (note), and III, *maamar* 1.

3. Contrast Yeshayahu Maori's criteria for distinguishing *peshat* from *derash*, translated in *Tradition* 21:3 (Fall 1984) p. 41: "1) whether the explanation is logically coherent; 2) whether it fits the context, and 3) whether it is compatible with the grammar of the language." It is unclear how these criteria would enable the midrash about Rivka to be classified as *derash* rather than *peshat*.

4. BT *Berachot* 33b, "Everything is in the hands of Heaven except for the fear of Heaven," and many similar statements, and see *Rambam*, *Hilchot Teshuvah*, ch. 5.

Chapter Four

THE SEEDS OF ENSLAVEMENT

In the previous chapter, we proposed *economy* as one of three criteria for gauging *peshat*. To the extent that the interpretation does not necessitate the introduction of new elements and data not indicated in the text, it is closer to *peshat*.

There is, however, another form of economy very different from the above. It may involve introducing new elements, but results in the explication of a number of disparate texts; hence the economy. The more texts elucidated, the more questions answered by one assumption—the greater the likelihood that the explanation is, in fact, *peshat*.

Perhaps the most outstanding example of this type of economy in interpretation, is the hypothesis that Yosef's sojourn in Egypt coincided with the rule of the Hyksos. The Hyksos were a tribe of mixed Semitic and Hurrian shepherd-warriors who conquered and ruled Egypt for a century sometime in the Patriarchal age. Josephus already mentions them, in the name of an Egyptian writer, and modern historians and archeologists accept their reign as historical fact.[1] The only question is, did Hyksos rule coincide with Yosef's rise to power in Egypt, or did it not? Here the internal evidence of the Torah is overwhelming: no fewer than six passages in

Bereishit and *Shemot* are best or solely explained by reference to Hyksos rule:

1) "Yosef was taken down to Egypt, and Potifar, minister of executions, *an Egyptian*, purchased him" (*Bereishit* 39:1). One would hardly need to identify a high official in Egypt as "an Egyptian," were it not that, under Hyksos rule, a native-born minister was an anomaly. We choose to translate *sar hatabachim* as "minister of executions" rather than chief cook, because the prison system was within his purview (40:3–4, 41:10). Why appoint an Egyptian as chief executioner? So that the hatred of the people be focused on him rather than on his Hyksos overlords. Much the same consideration prompted Polish landowners to appoint Jews as tax-collectors.

2) "He gave him Osnat the daughter of Poti Fera, priest of On, as a wife" (41:45). The Egyptians could not even eat together with the Hebrews "because it was an abomination to the Egyptians" (43:32), so how could they marry them? Rather, Asnat was not an Egyptian but a daughter of the Hyksos ruling class—itself foreign—which had no taboos against foreigners.

3) "Yosef recognized his brothers, but they did not recognize him" (42:8). Were Yosef a foreigner in an otherwise Egyptian court, the brothers would have made a special effort to note just who was this official with singularly non-Egyptian Semitic features. As it was, as a minister in a quasi-Semitic Hyksos government his origins attracted no attention.

4) "The news reached Pharaoh's house that Yosef's brothers had come, and it was welcomed by Pharaoh and his servants" (45:16). The non-Egyptian rulers welcomed the arrival of more Semites, as reinforcements.

5) "So that you dwell in the land of Goshen, for all shepherds are an abomination to the Egyptians" (46:34). Goshen was "the best part of the country" (47:6), and why would the Egyptians give it to those they abominated? Rather, the Hyksos, themselves shepherds, ruled the country, and they took the best parts for themselves and their allies.

6) "A new king arose in Egypt who knew not Yosef" (*Shemot* 1:8). A new, Egyptian, dynasty arose which threw out the Hyksos.[2] Following standard practice, it blotted out all memory of the previous rulers and administration.

Much of the above, particularly 1) and 6), has already been remarked upon by modern commentators. We will introduce, however, an additional hypothesis: Potifar, Yosef's master, was an Egyptian, but his *wife was a Hyksos*.[3] Perhaps, as with Yosef and Osnat in *Bereishit* 41:45, the practice was to give non-Hyksos ministers a wife from the ruling circles—if only to keep watch over them.[4]

This explains the astonishing latitude Potifar's wife gave herself in speaking about, and to, her husband. "She called the men of her house (*anshei beitah*)[5] and told them, 'See, he brought us a Hebrew (*ish ivri*) to ridicule us'" (*Bereishit* 39:14). When Potifar returned, "She spoke to him in the same way: 'The Hebrew slave you brought us came to ridicule [or: have relations with] me.'" It is remarkable for a high official's wife to express such disdain for her husband, let alone to her servants, and inconceivable that she class herself together with the latter, "he brought *us*..." Rather, "men of her house" means men of her *family*. She called in her

Hyksos relatives to complain about her Egyptian husband.

This is the sting in her accusation: "He brought us an *ish ivri* to ridicule us." *Ivri* means one who came from over (*me'eiver*) the Euphrates River, and can refer to any Semite.[6] Potifar, the Egyptian, had made a point of buying a Semitic slave in order to ridicule and degrade the part-Semitic Hyksos in whose government he served!

Potifar was furious, but not at Yosef. Had he entertained the possibility that his wife was telling the truth, he would have executed Yosef, and certainly not have placed him in the highest-quality prison (39:20) and continued to look after his welfare (40:4). But as a lone Egyptian in a Hyksos court, his hands were tied. He could not free Yosef without further incurring the wrath of his wife's family, who were closer to the center of power than he was. Yosef knew this full well, and so did not ask the chief cup-bearer to intercede with Potifar on his behalf, but only with Pharaoh (40:14).

Is all this historical fact? The question cannot be answered and is beside the point. What is important is that we have developed a strong and legitimate *peshat* that reflects the complexity that is characteristic of true events. The wider significance of the Hyksos connection is that it reveals the intrinsic fragility of Israel's foothold in Egypt: the Hyksos were a foreign graft in Egypt destined to be rejected, and with their overthrow, the reaction against Israel was only a matter of time. The rise to power of Yosef under a Hyksos regime contained within it the seeds of Israel's enslavement.

Notes

1. *Against Apion*, book 1, ch. 14, and see also chs. 15, 26–
    31. The details, however, of Josephus' account of the Hyk-
    sos are not factual; see *Encyclopaedia Judaica*, *s.v.* He-
    brew, Hyksos.

2. The "mixed multitude" (*eirev rav*) in *Shemot* 12:38
    would include the remnants of the Hyksos left in Egypt
    after their overthrow.

3. This casts her infatuation with Yosef in a new light, both
    being non-Egyptians.

4. Another possibility is that he married her as a means of
    gaining access to the ruling circles. In either case, Potifar
    ignored his own people's taboos against social intercourse
    with foreigners.

5. Not to be confused with *anshei habayit*, "men of the
    house" (servants) in v. 11, and see *Chibah Yeteirah* to
    Bereishit 15:3.

6. See *Shemot* 2:11. "...and he saw an Egyptian man hitting
    a Hebrew man (*ish ivri*) from his brethren." Why was it
    necessary to specify "from his brethren"? Because there
    were other Hebrews in Egypt who were not Israelites.

HALACHA

Chapter Five

WOMEN AND KADDISH

There has been a tendency in recent years to use halachic arguments to buttress what are essentially ideological positions. A recent example of this is Rabbi Reuven Fink's article, "The Recital of Kaddish by Women,"[1] which he concludes by stating,

> It would therefore seem that an attempt to "improve" or alter our sacred traditions and halachic precepts is in re-ality not a positive move but a negative one. Given the *zeitgeist* that prevails today, which serves as the impetus to change our time-honored laws concerning modesty, identity and role differentiation, this change in both pernicious and dangerous...Tampering with the synagogue's customary practices is clearly a step fraught with great danger.[2]

The core of R. Fink's article is an attempt to show that the *psak* of my grandfather, R. Yosef Eliyahu Henkin זצ"ל, which permitted women to say *kaddish yatom* in *shul* from the women's section simultaneously with men saying kaddish, and my own elucidation thereof, was wrong and should not be followed. Quite to the contrary, *Rav* Henkin's approach to this issue reflected the classical halachic intuition and sensitivity that he was legendary for, and his *psak* remains as halachically valid and relevant today as the day it was written nearly 50 years ago.

The author raises three major objections:

First, kaddish requires a *minyan* of ten men. The women's section is a separate domain from that of the men's section, and the girl is therefore saying kaddish only in front of the women, who do not constitute the requisite quorum for the kaddish to be recited.[3]

I discussed this objection at length in my Responsa *Bnei Banim* II, no. 7. Following the views of the *rishonim* in *Eiruvin* (72a) and elsewhere, the great majority of women's sections today are, for the purposes of a quorum, extensions of the men's section; i.e., nine men in the men's section and one man behind the *mechitzah* in the women's section would constitute a *minyan*. There are two rationales for this: 1) In the absence of a floor-to-ceiling partition or separating wall which is rare today, the common roof unites the two into one room, following the opinion of *Hagahot haSemak*,[4] *Or Zarua*,[5] *R. Yehonatan*[6] and others; and 2) the women's section is functionally subordinate (*beteilah, nigreret*) to the men's section (*Ramban*,[7] *Rashba*,[8] *Shulchan Aruch*[9]).

A woman saying kaddish behind the *mechitzah* when there are ten men in the men's section, therefore, is indeed saying kaddish with a *minyan*. This explains, as well, the permission given by many authorities for a woman to recite *birkat hagomel* in the women's section, with the men in the men's section answering, even though *birkat hagomel* also requires the presence of a *minyan*.[10]

The second objection is a historical one. My grandfather had to explain how he could counter the halachic precedent of hundreds of years' standing which prohibited women from saying kaddish in the synagogue. This he did with characteristically simple logic:

> In the time of the *achronim* who discussed this, the custom was that one person would say kaddish—and therefore it was not for the *na'arah* to say kaddish—for such was the way of the *rishonim*, that the person saying kaddish would say it at the prayer-leader's desk (*lifnei hateivah*), and it certainly is not proper to allow the *na'arah* to come to the prayer-leader's desk as a *shaliach tzibur*, even for kaddish alone. But now that everyone says [kaddish] in his place and many are those who recite [kaddish], it should not be totally rejected. I have already written that it is correct for her to stand behind the *mechitzah* [and recite kaddish].[11]

This, when combined with my observation that she can recite kaddish simultaneously with the male mourners in a quiet voice, and thus not be heard at all in the men's section, meets virtually all objections of the *achronim*:

1) The objection that the change in *minhag* would undermine established custom (Resp. *Chavot Yair*),[12] or lead to confusion and to a woman acting as a *shaliach tzibur* or being counted as part of a *minyan* (Resp. *Torah liShmah*).[13] The conspicuousness of a woman saying kaddish in such a fashion is virtually nil and the change in custom negligible—the men say kaddish exactly as before—as compared with her being the only person saying kaddish in the synagogue, even if she is behind the *mechitzah* or, *kal vachomer*, in a *minyan* in her home in full view of the men (the latter case is the one discussed by *Chavot Yair* and *Torah liShmah*). Nor is a woman who remains in the women's section likely to be confused with a *shaliach tzibur* or counted in a *minyan*.

2) the objection that listening to her may violate the prohibition of *kol be'ishah* (*Mateh Efraim*,[14] *Elef laMateh*[15]), and that her presence would be immodest and distract the men (*Aseh Lecha Rav*[16] and others). When she recites kaddish simultaneously with the men the principle "*trei kali lo mishtamei*,"[17] two voices are not heard at once, applies, and if she is inaudible there is of course no *kol ishah* to start with. Nor is there immodesty or visual distraction when she remains behind the *mechitzah*.

R. Fink, however, casts doubt on the historical accuracy of distinguishing between past and present *minhag*, and challenges:

> Rabbi Yehuda Herzl Henkin's assertion that all of the early negative decisions regarding a woman's saying kaddish were based solely upon the different practice than that of today...would certainly be enhanced by scholarly evidence showing the historical era and regions where the new custom, of many people saying kaddish in unison, began. If he could demonstrate that...local custom was for one person only to say the kaddish, he might then have a tenable argument.[18]

Substitute "Rabbi Yosef Eliyahu Henkin," who first made the assertion, in place of "Rabbi Yehuda Herzl Henkin" in the above paragraph, and one gets an idea of the breathtaking nature of such a challenge.

It can be stated unequivocally that in every important Ashkenazic community from the Middle Ages through well into the 19th century, the custom was for one person only to say the kaddish. The Sephardic custom of mourners reciting kaddish in unison began to be adopted by European Ashkenazic communities only in the late 19th century. As recently as 1917, *Otzar Dinim uMinha-*

gim referred to it as the custom of the Sephardim and of the "Ashkenazic communities in America."[19]

In 1854, Resp. *Binyan Tzion* wrote that "in all the regions of Germany and Poland there is not found even one community" which follows the Sephardic practice "except for that which novelty-seekers, who don't care about the customs of Israel, have instituted."[20] Prior to that, in 1800, Resp. *Chatam Sofer*[21] defended the accepted Ashkenazic practice of only one person saying the kaddish, against R. Yaakov Emden's recommendation of the Sephardic one. Moreover, the same authorities who oppose a daughter's saying kaddish in the synagogue discuss the Halacha of who takes precedence over whom among men seeking to say kaddish, but omit any mention of the possibility of reciting kaddish in unison: see Resp. *Knesset Yechezkel*[22] (pub. 1630); Resp. *Shevut Yaakov*[23] (pub. 1711); Resp. *Teshuvah meAhavah*[24] (pub. 1715); and *Mateh Efraim*[25] (pub. 1835). *Elef haMagen*, which does mention the possibility, is a later commentary on the *Mateh Efraim* and dates from 1908.

The third objection is that other contemporary authorities and/or Sephardic ones do not permit a woman to say kaddish. This is not an especially strong argument. *Rav* Henkin, as a *posek hador*, was fully competent to issue his own *psak*, particularly for Ashkenazim.

Moreover, it is not clear of what relevance to our question are the Sephardic *poskim* the author cites as objecting to a woman's saying kaddish in spite of Sephardic custom that mourners recite kaddish in unison. The role and participation of Sephardic women in Jewish life is very different from that of Ashkenazic women. As a *rav* in Bet Shean in Israel, I found that some Sephardic synagogues had no women's section at all, and the occasional woman or two who came to *shul* simply stood at the back or the sides of the men's section.[26]

We do not know, therefore, what circumstances the *Sdei Chemed* was referring to when he prohibited a woman's saying kaddish,[27] and whether the woman would have been standing behind a *mechitzah*. Resp. *Torah liShmah* and the present-day *Aseh Lecha Rav* explicitly deal with women who say kaddish in full view of the men. *Piskei Uziel*, on the other hand, prohibits women from saying kaddish on principle, explaining that kaddish is for men only.[28] This is not the Ashkenazic view: even *Chavot Yair* accepted a daughter's saying kaddish in theory and prohibited it only for secondary reasons, while *Shevut Yaakov* permitted it outright in special circumstances.[29]

We are left where we started: at issue is essentially a question of policy and not of *issur veheter*. In this context my grandfather's words bear repeating:

> It is known that were it not for kaddish, many would refrain from teaching prayer to their sons and would not come to synagogue. When they come because of kaddish they also come a bit closer to Judaism the rest of the year, and for this reason itself one should not rebuff the *na'arot* either, since it fosters closeness to Judaism.[30]

On questions of policy, others may legitimately disagree. We should support any rabbi who declares, "While such a practice may be technically according to Halacha, in my opinion, it would have dangerous consequences in my community and so I will not permit it"—although I would urge careful consideration of my grandfather's approach even in the white heat of current controversy.[31] What must be avoided is the confusion of Halacha with polemics.

Notes

1. In *Journal of Halacha and Contemporary Society*, Spring 1996, pp. 23–37. This chapter originally appeared as a letter to the editor in the Fall 1996 issue, pp. 97–102.

2. *Ibid.*, Spring 1996, p. 37.

3. *Ibid.*, p. 30.

4. *Mitzvah* 282, *Hilchot Eiruvin*, note 5.

5. Part 2, sec. 172.

6. BT *Eiruvin* 72b.

7. See *Bnei Banim*, II, pp. 27–8.

8. Resp. *HaRashba*, I, no. 96.

9. *Orach Chayim* 55:19

10. See *Bnei Banim*, *loc. cit.*

11. *Kitvei haGri"a Henkin*, vol. 2, p. 6. The term *"na'arah"* refers to a girl before marriage; however, my grandfather permitted married women as well to recite the kaddish. Cf. *Ibid.*, pp. 3–5, "kaddish by a daughter," and Resp. *Igrot Moshe* cited below in the following chapter, note 4.

12. No. 222.

13. *Orach Chayim*, no. 27.

14. *Dinei Kaddish Yatom, sha'ar* 4:8.

15. *Ibid.*

16. Vol. 5, pp. 234–6.

17. BT *Rosh HaShanah* 27a.

18. *Loc. cit.*, p. 34.

19. *S.v.* Kaddish, *s. s. v. Minyan hakaddishim.*

20. I, no. 122.

21. *Orach Chayim*, no. 159, *s. v. Od ani.*

22. *Yoreh Deah*, end.

23. II, no. 93.

24. No. 229.

25. *Sha'ar* 2.

26. R. Shalom Mashash, Sephardic Chief Rabbi of Jerusalem and formerly Chief Rabbi of Casablanca, writes that in Morocco women generally did not attend synagogue, even on Yom Kippur, and that few synagogues had women's sections; see Resp. *Shemesh uMagen*, nos. 55(4) and 72(3).

27. *Pe'at haSadeh, ma'arechet aveulut*, par. 160.

28. *She'eilot haZeman*, no. 3.

29. Both *Chavot Yair* and *Shevut Yaakov* dealt with the question of a daughter saying kaddish at a *minyan* in her home; in the case of the *Shevut Yaakov* she was four years old.

30. *Kitvei haGri"a Henkin, loc. cit.*

31. See *Bnei Banim*, I, no. 37, sec. 12, on the importance of accurately presenting what is halachically permitted and what is forbidden.

Chapter Six

WOMEN, KADDISH, AND THE HALACHIC PROCESS

In his reply to my letter, R. Fink largely ignores my halachic arguments, preferring instead to reiterate his claim that "the decision of *Rav* Yosef Eliyahu Henkin [with regard to women saying kaddish] was unacceptable to and rejected by his contemporaries."[1] This reflects a misunderstanding of the halachic process which transcends the question of women saying *kaddish yatom*; in American idiom, it can be compared to an umpire seeking to call the game without realizing there are innings left to be played.

Innumerable halachic controversies continue over many generations. In the Talmud, a statement is often made by one authority and objected to by an *amora* of another generation; the objection is then met by a rabbi of still a later period and so forth, until a final decision is reached, if at all. The same applies to arguments among *rishonim* and *achronim* in which the give-and-take may span hundreds of years.

What constitutes final resolution of a question is a complex affair. Consensus may be reached among *poskim*, or communal practice may be determinative. Often a decision is rendered by an authority whose rulings are considered binding, such as the *Shulchan*

Aruch or *Rama*. In any case, resolution is not reached until all components are in place, and even seemingly closed questions are subject to reopening when new evidence is introduced. Such evidence typically consists of authoritative opinions previously overlooked, new interpretations of and proofs from *chaza"l* and *poskim*, compelling logical arguments or changed circumstances.

Obviously, a higher order of proof is necessary to differ with a ruling of the *Shulchan Aruch* than to challenge an uncodified *minhag*, and I make no attempt to list all the factors involved. It should also be noted that justified challenges, even of *minhagim*, are relatively rare. Nevertheless, critique and reevaluation of earlier rulings are the common activity of *poskim* in every generation.

In the discussion of women and kaddish, we can ascertain at least five stages:

The first stage consisted of the raising of the issue over three hundred years ago by Responsa *Chavot Yair* and subsequent authorities, and their rulings.[2]

The second stage began with my grandfather's noting the changed circumstances in synagogue practices regarding *kaddish yatom* today as opposed to in the time of the above, and the conclusions he reached. R. Fink's attempt to date the change in Ashkenazic *minhag* from individual to group recital of kaddish as occurring in the early nineteenth century rather than in the late nineteenth century as I had written, is of no consequence, as even his date is still well over a century after the *Chavot Yair*. Also, the *Kitzur Shulchan Aruch* 26:18, first printed in 1864 in Hungary, does not say a "long-standing" custom as R. Fink writes but only a "widespread" one.[3] Nor is the group recital of *kaddish derabbanan* or the exceptional case of a large number of mourners in the synagogue, when there are not enough *kaddishim* to go around, proof of a change in the normal *minhag*.[4]

The third stage consisted of the objections to my grandfather's *psak* raised by some of his contemporaries and subsequent *poskim*. R. Fink is mistaken in thinking that the halachic process stopped here. In particular, he notes Responsa *Minchat Yitzchak*'s disagreement with my grandfather but without mentioning R. Weiss' rationale, that there is no *minyan* present in the *ezrat nashim*, or that I wrote *Bnei Banim*, II, no. 7 explicitly to answer this objection. In halachic methodology, an objection, when met, may be rendered moot under the assumption that the objector himself would have concurred had he seen the explanation.

The fourth stage consists of the response to these objections by my grandfather, by myself in *Bnei Banim* and elsewhere, and perhaps by others.

The fifth stage will be the response of current and future *poskim* to the defense of my grandfather's position.

The issue of women saying *kaddish yatom*, therefore, will continue to be debated on its merits, and until its final resolution rabbis and communities may rely on my grandfather's cogent *psak* and reasoning. No less important may be the response of the community, in the form of *puk chazi mai ama davar*. Different communities may also adopt different stances, and there is already evidence of this occurring.

Notes

1. In the *Journal of Halacha and Contemporary Society*, Fall 1996, pp. 107–8, in response to my first letter; see previous chapter. The *Journal* subsequently declined to print this second letter.

2. See dates of publication listed in the previous chapter.

3. *Kitzur Shulchan Aruch* cites *Pitchei Teshuvah* (published 1836) to *Yoreh Deah* 376, no. 6, which, however, does not say the custom was widespread but only that the author of Resp. *Divrei Rivot* instituted it in his community. Perhaps group recital of kaddish was adopted in Hungary before reaching Poland or Germany: see Resp. *Binyan Tzion*, I, no. 122, quoted in the previous chapter.

4. In exceptional circumstances, *Chavot Yair* might agree to a woman's saying kaddish even in the absence of other mourners; in responsum no. 222 he deals with the question of a daughter's saying kaddish daily for the entire mourning period, but not with the occasional or irregular recital of kaddish on her part. Cf. Resp. *Igrot Moshe, Orach Chayim*, V, no. 12 (2): "In all generations it was customary that occasionally...a female mourner would enter the *beit midrash* to say kaddish" i.e., with a *minyan*. His question there is whether it is proper for her to do so without a *mechitzah*, even occasionally; that she can say kaddish at all is taken for granted.

Chapter Seven

WOMEN AND *MEGILLAH* READING

Three factors enter into a halachic decision. The first is the optimal, or "pure," Halacha determined from the sources alone.

The second is the *metzi'ut*, "reality," the situation on the ground.

To bridge any gap between the two comes the third element, *hora'ah*, literally "ruling." This employs many principles Halacha itself provides, such as the difference between ruling *lechatchilah*, "initially" and *bedi'eved*, "after the fact." Or, *sha'at hadchak*, "pressing circumstances." Or, the obligation to keep quiet, in certain cases, when one knows one won't be listened to or when the ruling is likely to be misunderstood or misused. Women's reading the Purim *megillah* for other women, an issue of some recent controversy,[1] will serve to illustrate some of the complexities of both Halacha and *hora'ah*.

Three halachic approaches are found in the *rishonim* on the question of the obligation of women to read the *megillah* on Purim:

1. Men and women are equally obligated in *kri'at hamegillah* and, therefore, either sex can read for the other.

2. Men are obligated to read the *megillah* but women are only obligated to *hear* it read; a lesser obligation. Therefore, a woman cannot read for men, following

the halachic principle that only one equally obligated by a *mitzvah* can perform that *mitzvah* for others and thereby discharge their obligation.[2]

3. Men and women are equally obligated to read the *megillah* but, *nevertheless*, a woman may not read for men.

These *shitot* (halachic positions) can be referred to as **A**, **B**, and **C**.

Shitah **A**, that men and women are equal and interchangeable as regards the reading of the *megillah*, is that of *Rashi*,[3] *Rambam*,[4] and many other early authorities.[5] It is based on the statement in *Megillah* (4a), "R. Yehoshua ben Levi said, women are obligated in *kri'at hamegillah*, because they too were part of the same miracle." Similarly, in *Archin* (3a), "'All are qualified to read the *megillah*'...[this comes] to include women."

Shitah **B** is based on the *Tosefta Megillah* (2:4), according to which women, in regard to the *megillah* reading, are not interchangeable with men: "All are obligated to read the *megillah*, *kohanim*, Levites, and Israelites...[but] women are exempt and do not enable the many [=men] to fulfill their obligation." While view **A** rejects or amends this *Tosefta* as contradicting the Gemara, **B** reconciles the two sources: the Gemara refers to the obligation of women to hear the reading of the *megillah*, while the *Tosefta* exempts them from reading the *megillah*. Since men have the *mitzvah* of reading but women do not, men cannot fulfill their *mitzvah* by having a woman read it to them.

This is the opinion of the Gaonic work *Halachot Gedolot* as found in our editions:

> Women, slaves, and minors are exempt from reading the
> *megillah* but are obligated to hear it (*chayavim
> bemashma)*. Why? Because they were all endangered by
> [Haman's plan] "to destroy, kill, and wipe out [the Jew-
> ish people]" (Esther 3:13); since they were all endan-
> gered, they are all obligated to hear it.[6]

This opinion of *Halachot Gedolot* is cited by the *Tosafot*
in *Archin* (3a)[7] and by *Raviah*,[8] *Mordechai*,[9] and many
other *rishonim*.[10]

Shitah **C**, on the other hand, while accepting the view
of **A** that men and women are equally obligated to read
the *megillah*, nevertheless follows **B** in prohibiting
women from reading it for men. It interprets the *Tosefta*
as prohibiting such reading on extraneous grounds.
According to *Sefer Mitzvot Gadol*,

> Even though women are obligated in the reading of the
> *megillah*, they do not discharge males from their obliga-
> tion...*Megillah* is different in that it is like the reading of
> the Torah; therefore, she doesn't discharge a man from
> his obligation.[11]

Just as women can, in principle, be called up to the
reading of the Torah in a men's *minyan* but this has been
forbidden in practice,[12] so too, they may not read the
megillah for men.

A slightly different explanation is brought by *Sefer
haKolbo* and *Orchot Chayim* in the name of an earlier
rishon: "The author of *Aseret haDibrot*[13] wrote that
when reading [the *megillah*] women do not enable men
to fulfill their obligation; the reason is *kol be'ishah
ervah*,"[14] i.e., while technically permissible, it is immodest for women to read the *megillah* for men.

It is important for our discussion to note that *Halachot Gedolot*, even though identified above as position **B**, is apparently seen by a number of *rishonim* as subscribing rather to opinion **C**. The *Tur* writes in his name, "Even though women are obligated in *mikra megillah*, they do not enable males to fulfill their obligation."[15] This is the same language as used by *Sefer Mitzvot Gadol*, i.e., women are equally obligated, but nevertheless may not read for men.

Proof that such an opinion is indeed attributed to *Halachot Gedolot* can be found in *Tosfot haRosh* to *Sukkah* (38a):[16]

> ...Or else [the reason why women cannot say *birkat hamazon* for men is that] it is dishonorable (*zila beho milta*) for men to have women enable them to fulfill their obligation, just like *megillah* where women are obligated [but] *Halachot Gedolot* said that women do not enable the many to fulfill their obligation.

Were the view ascribed here to *Halachot Gedolot* that of **B**, that the *mitzvah* of *megillah* for women is less than and different from that of men, there would be no cause to compare it with *zila beho milta* in *birkat hamazon*—in fact, just the opposite, since *Tosfot haRosh* argues that women's inability to say *birkat hamazon* for men is *not* proof that her obligation is less than theirs!

As a rule, *Tosfot haRosh* restates and occasionally amplifies the views of the regular *Tosafot*,[17] who in *Sukkah* (38a) write in similar fashion:

> ...Or else [women cannot say *birkat hamazon* for men] because it is dishonorable for the many (*zila beho milta*), for it is [like] *megillah* in which women are obligated

[but] *Halachot Gedolot* explained that women do not enable the many to fulfill their obligation in *megillah*.

This *Tosfot haRosh*, then, is proof that the phrase
"women do not enable the many" in the parallel *Tosafot*
in *Sukkah* refers to women reading for men, and that the
view attributed to *Halachot Gedolot* by this *Tosafot* is **C**
and not **B**.[18] Further indication of this is found in *Sefer
haAgudah* in *Sukkah*: "*Ri* explained that women do not
enable men to fulfill their obligation of *megillah*, even
though they and men are equally obligated (*chayavot
ka'anashim*)," i.e., opinion **C**. "*Ri*" is the preeminent
Tosafist R. Isaac of Dampierre, and there is no doubt
that *Sefer haAgudah* in *Sukkah* is summarizing the
discussion of the *Tosafot* on location in *Sukkah*.

Why is this important for our question of women
reading the *megillah* for other women? Because the 18th
century authority R. Netaniel Weil, in his commentary
on the Rosh called *Korban Netanel*, assumed that the
opinion attributed to *Halachot Gedolot* by the *Tosafot* in
Sukkah is **B**, that women are less obligated than are men.
This led him to interpret the *Tosafot* as ruling that a
woman may read the *megillah* only for herself but not
for a group of other women:

> That which the *Tosafot* in *Sukkah* 38a wrote, "...Or else
> [women cannot say *birkat hamazon* for men] because it
> is dishonorable for the many, for it is [like] *megillah* in
> which women are obligated [but] *Halachot Gedolot* ex-
> plained that women do not enable the many to fulfill
> their obligation in *megillah*," that is to say that a woman
> may not enable many *women* to fulfill their obligation,
> because it is dishonorable for them [to have the *megillah*
> read to them by a women]. But as far as reading for men,
> *even without this reason they cannot do so*, not even one

woman for one man, because they [women] are not obligated [to read the *megillah*].[19]

His view is cited by the *Mishnah Berurah*,[20] the normally authoritative commentary on the *Shulchan Aruch, Orach Chayim*. In this case, however, neither the *Korban Netanel* nor the *Mishnah Berurah* knew of the *Tosfot haRosh* on *Sukkah*, which was not yet in print.[21] Had they seen it, they would not have written as they did.

It can thus be stated categorically that there is no opinion in the Talmud or *rishonim* that prohibits a woman from reading the *megillah* for herself or for any number of other women.[22] Moreover, as opposed to many innovations in women's prayer groups which, even if not explicitly forbidden, are at the least not anticipated by any authority, women's *megillah* readings are a clearly implied halachic option.

Nonetheless, there are a number of possible reasons why women should attend the regular *megillah* readings by men in the synagogue, all things being equal. These include: the preference (*hidur*) of having as many participants as possible in one large public reading rather than fragmented into smaller ones;[23] the initial (*lechatchilah*) obligation to read the *megillah* in the presence of ten men[24] or ten women,[25] which is often possible only at the synagogue reading; questions as to the proper blessing to be recited;[26] and the general desirability of performing a *mitzvah* sooner rather than later.[27]

All things are often not equal, however:

1) It is often impossible for women to properly hear from the *ezrat nashim*. The inaudibility of even one

word from the *megillah* reading means that the listener has not fulfilled her obligation.[28]

2) Women, and particularly mothers, are often unable to come to the synagogue at the specified times.

For these and other reasons there has emerged a widespread practice to have a second *megillah* reading for women, and in such circumstances it is entirely proper for a woman—or women—to read the *megillah*. Even women who have already heard the *megillah* read, and have thus discharged their own obligation, can read for other women in a second reading.[29] In fact, when the alternative is to have a teenage boy read the *megillah* for a group of learned women, it may be close to being *zila beho milta* for the women not to read the *megillah* themselves.[30]

Notes

1. In February 1997, the Queens, NY *Vaad Harabbonim* included women's *megillah* readings in a list of prohibited activities. Shortly afterwards, a women's *megillah* reading scheduled at Yeshiva University's Stern College for Women was cancelled by the administration.

2. Mishna in *Rosh haShanah* 29a; *Rambam, Hilchot Shofar* 2:2; *Shulchan Aruch, Orach Chayim* 589:1.

3. BT *Archin* 3a, *s.v. le'atuyei nashim*.

4. *Hilchot Megillah* 1:1.

5. *Sefer haMeorot, Riaz* in *Shaltei haGiborim, Ritva, Meiri* and *Nimukei Yosef*, all on BT *Megillah* 4a; *Or Zarua*, pt. 2, no. 368. This is also, apparently, the opinion of *Rashba* (ed. Dimitrovski) to *Megillah* 4a, who rejects the *Tosefta*. These *rishonim*, together with *Rashi*, state explicitly that

women can read for men. Others imply as much by quoting R. Yehoshua ben Levi or mentioning women's obligation to read the *megillah*, without qualification: see *Rambam* in previous note and also *Rif* and *Raban* to *Megillah* 4a; *Shibolei haLeket* 198; *Ohel Moed, Dinei Megillah*, 1 (vol. 2, p. 108).

6. *Halachot Gedolot*, Venice edition, p. 80 (Hildesheimer edition, p. 406).

7. *S.v. le'atuyei nashim.*

8. Ch. 569.

9. To *Megillah* 4a, *remez* 778.

10. *Sefer haItur* (*Aseret haDibrot*), *Hilchot Megillah s.v. mi koreh*; *Sefer haEshkol* (ed. Auerbach), pt. 2, p. 30; *Sefer haNiyar; Rosh, Sefer haAgudah* and *Ran* (on the *Rif*) to *Megillah* 4a; *Rabbeinu Yerucham* 10:2. *Sefer haEshkol* and *Raviah* write that the author of *Halachot Gedolot* had a different version of *Megillah* 4a: instead of "women are obligated in *kri'at* (reading) *megillah*," his text of the Talmud read "women are obligated in *mashma* (hearing) *megillah*," This is also stated by the *Mordechai*, who follows *Raviah* (the emendation printed in the *Mordechai*, בה"ג פרש in place of בה"ג גרס, is unwarranted).

This leads to a difficult question concerning the blessing to be recited before a *megillah* reading by, or on behalf of, women. According to *Rashi, Rambam et al.* the blessing is certainly "*al mikra megillah*," ("on the reading of the *megillah*"), the same as a man's. *Raviah* and *Mordechai*, on the other hand, following the view of *Halachot Gedolot*, write that it is "*al mashma megillah*" ("on the hearing of the *megillah*"). The *Rama* in *Orach Chayim* 689:2 accepts a variation of this and writes, "There are those who say that if a woman reads for herself she makes the blessing '*lishmo'a megillah*' ('to hear the *megillah*'), since she is not obligated to read." Ashkenazic practice is indeed for women to make the blessing "*lishmo'a megillah*" (*Rama* and others) or "*lishmo'a mikra megillah*" (*Chayei Adam* and *Mishnah Brerurah;* cf. *Rabbenu Chananel* to *Megillah* 4a).

On what basis do we prefer the blessing according to *Raviah* to the one according to *Rashi* and *Rambam*? Were it not for the established *minhag*, we might well rule that women should make no blessing at all, because of the *safek* of which version to use. The difficulty is independent of the question of whether or not women should read the *megillah* for themselves and applies equally to the blessings made when a man reads the *megillah* a second time for women. Cf. Resp. *Teshuvot veHanhagot*, I, *Orach Chayim*, no. 403.

11. *Smag, Hilchot Megillah.* This comparison to reading the Torah is also found in *Sefer haEshkol* and in R. Avraham Min haHar on BT *Megillah* 19b.

12. BT *Megillah* 23a.

13. Not found in our editions of *Sefer haItur.*

14. *Sefer haKolbo,* ch. 45, and *Orchot Chayim, Hilchot Megillah* par. 2; the interpretation is also mentioned in *Sefer haEshkol.* On whether a woman's reading the Torah with cantillation constitutes *kol be'ishah*, see my Resp. *Bnei Banim,* II, no. 10, pp. 38-39.

If women may not read the *megillah* for men only because of extraneous reasons, then a man read to by a woman has *bedi'eved* fulfilled his obligation, and this is indeed the opinion of R. Avraham Min haHar cited in note 11 above. Also, see R. David Auerbach, *Halichot Beitah*, p. 339, par. 12, regarding *kol be'ishah*. However, *Sefer haEshkol* both quotes *Halachot Gedolot* that women are obligated only to hear the *megillah* and at the same time gives the reasons of similarity to Torah readings and *kol be'ishah*. According to this, the similarity to Torah readings and *kol be'ishah* are not extraneous but are the reasons why *chaza"l* freed women of the obligation to read the *megillah* in the first place, to prevent them from reading for men (*"lehachi tiknu shelo totzi anashim"*), and thus a man read to by a woman has not fulfilled his obligation even *bedi'eved*. This resolves the conceptual difficulty in distinguishing between the obligations of men and women in spite of their all having been "part of the same miracle"; cf. *Aruch haShulchan, Orach Chayim* 689, par. 5 and *Sefer Bnei Tzion* (Lichtman), vol. 4, 271:2 (3), pp. 120b–121a.

15. *Tur, Orach Chayim* 689, and cf. *Meiri, loc. cit.*

16. *S. v. be'emet amru.*

17. There is thus no contradiction between *Tosfot haRosh*'s restatement here of *Tosafot*'s version of *Halachot Gedolot* and his quoting a different version in his own *Psakim*, cited in note 10 above. See also *Bnei Banim*, I, p. 93.

18. That *Tosafot* in *Archin* 3a cite *Halachot Gedolot* as B is no proof that they do so in *Sukkah*. *Tosafot* in different tractates are often by different authors.

19. *Korban Netanel* on *Megillah*, ch. 1, par. *mem.*

20. *Orach Chayim* 689, in *Sha'ar haTziyun* 15. The *Aruch haShulchan, ad loc.*, however, ignores the *Korban Netanel*, and in 271, par. 5 understands the *Tosafot* in *Sukkah* as referring to women reading for men. On the relative authority of the *Mishnah Berurah* and *Aruch haShulchan*, see *Bnei Banim*, I, p. 22, note, and II, no. 5.

21. *Korban Netanel* was printed in 1766, *Mishnah Berurah* in 1883, and *Tosafot haRosh* to *Sukkah* in 1903.

22. There is a possible extra-Talmudic opinion to this effect attributed to the *Midrash Neelam* or *Zohar Chadash* on the book of Ruth. *Magen Avraham* on *Orach Chayim* 689, par. 6, paraphrases it as "a woman should not read [the *megillah* even] for herself, but hear it from men." However, *Biur haGra* quotes the language of the *Zohar Chadash* differently, and writes: "...that which is written in *Archin*, 'All are qualified etc. to include women,' means to enable [other] women to fulfill their obligation, and such is also written in the *Zohar Chadash*, Ruth 78b: 'Women are obligated in *mikra megillah*, but do not read to others [=men], but are required to hear it from the one who makes the blessings.'" The last phrase of the *Zohar Chadash* is unclear, and the connecting phrase used by the *Gra* "and such is *also* written" (*v'chen katuv*) indicates that he brings the *Zohar Chadash* in *support* of his preceding statement that "'to include women' means to enable [other] women to fulfill their obligation" and not in contradiction.

23. *"Be'rov am hadrat melech"* (Proverbs 14:28), "with many people [comes] splendor for the king [G-d]." Technically, however, this may not apply to women; see *Halichot Beitah, Petach haBayit*, ch. 25. Also, *"be'rov am hadrat melech"* applies equally to other prayers and blessings, and in communities which ignore it the year round in favor of small *minyanim* etc. it should not be selectively applied to women on Purim.

24. *Shulchan Aruch, Orach Chayim* 680:18.

25. Consensus of *achronim*, see *Halichot Beitah*, ch. 24, par. 17 and note 27.

26. See note 10 above.

27. *"Zerizim makdimim lemitzvot"* (BT *Pesachim* 4a), "the industrious perform the *mitzvot* early."

28. Unless the listener said the missed words out loud herself.

29. See *Halichot Beitah*, *Petach haBayit*, ch. 17, regarding the consensus of *achronim* on women's *areivut*.

30. See *Bnei Banim*, II, no. 10, p. 36–38 on the meaning of *kevod hatzibur*.

Chapter Eight

KOL ISHAH REVIEWED

In an article entitled "*Kol 'Isha*," Rabbi Saul J. Berman questions the commonly-accepted prohibition of men listening to a woman singing.[1]

Shmuel's statement "*Kol be'ishah ervah*" is mentioned in tractate *Berachot* (24a) in a discussion of *ervah* regarding reading the *Shema*, and again in *Kiddushin* (70a) in the context of exchanging greetings with a married woman. It is *not* mentioned in *Sotah* (48a) in the context of the following statement: "R. Yosef said, When men sing and women respond [in song], it is licentiousness (*pritzuta*); when women sing and men respond, it is like fire in kindling." Nor do the *Gaonim* mention *kol be'ishah ervah* in their discussion of R. Yosef's statement. R. Berman writes:

> This fact alone would have been sufficient to allow a conclusion...that Samuel's law is not a general proposition as to the sexually arousing character of a women's voice, but rather is a restriction on the recitation of *Shema* under circumstances where it is not possible to maintain proper concentration.[2]

This rather startling proposition is expanded upon in the article's following page:

...It is clear that the central concern with hearing a woman's voice is not its intrinsic sensuousness, but the purely functional concern that it might distract a man from his concentration on prayer or study. It is certainly significant that the sole contexts in which the law of *Kol 'Isha* is held applicable are ones which require some special degree of attentiveness, and in which distraction is of particular concern.

The author seems to, but can hardly, be claiming that the distraction is not of a sexual nature. First, *kol be'ishah ervah* itself *means* "a women's voice is a sexual excitement," as he himself translates.[3] Second, its mention in *Kiddushin* (70a) is outside any context of distraction. Third, if simple distraction was the issue, then a man's singing voice, or even music altogether, would also be an impediment to reciting *Shema*.

Clearly, the sexual element of *kol be'ishah* is operative; what needs to be clarified are the halachic disabilities or prohibitions stemming from this element. Specifically, one must understand the key discussion in *Berachot* (24a), which R. Berman neither explicates nor even quotes:

> R. Yitzchak said: An [uncovered] hand's-breadth is *ervah*. In what context? If regarding looking [at a woman], did not R. Sheshet say: ...Anyone who gazes even at a woman's little finger is as if he gazes at her private parts? Rather, regarding his wife and reading *Shema*.
> R. Chisda said: A woman's thigh is *ervah*, as is written...
> Shmuel said: A woman's voice is *ervah*, as is written...
> R. Sheshet said: A woman's hair is *ervah*, as is written...

Is Shmuel's statement that a woman's voice is *ervah* (and R. Sheshet's statement concerning hair) an extension of R. Yitzchak's dictum that an uncovered hand's-breadth of her skin is *ervah* as regards the reading of *Shema*? Or, does it rather refer to R. Sheshet's statement about gazing at women? If the latter, then what Shmuel is saying is that in the same way that gazing at a woman's little finger is tantamount to gazing at her private parts, so too, is attentively listening to her voice. The prohibition of doing so is general and has nothing specifically to do with reading *Shema*, and this is patently the source for many *rishonim* who omit both a woman's voice and her hair from the list of impediments to a man's reciting the *Shema*; including *Rambam*,[4] *Smag*,[5] *Ri*,[6] *Or Zarua*,[7] as well as Rabbeinu Tam.[8]

Other *rishonim* include hair in the list of impediments to reciting the *Shema* but omit voice; including *Piskei Rid*,[9] *Smak*,[10] *Rosh*[11] and *Tur*,[12] and this is the opinion of the *Shulchan Aruch*.[13] According to both these groups, listening to a women's voice for the purpose of enjoyment would be a prohibited form of sexual stimulation equivalent to gazing at her, unrelated to prayer or study.

Many other *rishonim*, on the other hand, view both Shmuel's and R. Sheshet's second dictum as referring back to R. Yitzchak's statement, i.e., in the same way that reading *Shema* is prohibited if a normally covered hand's-breadth of a woman's body is visible—even that of one's wife—so too, is it prohibited while seeing her uncovered hair or hearing her voice. These *rishonim* include R. Hai Gaon,[14] *Rabbeinu Chananel*,[15] *Ravyah*,[16] *Ravad*,[17] *Rashba*[18] and many others.

We can now see the irrelevancy of Shmuel's dictum *kol be'ishah ervah* in *Berachot* to R. Yosef's criticism of responsive singing at feasts in *Sotah*. For those *rishonim* who apply *kol be'ishah ervah* to reading the *Shema*, R. Yosef is clearly not dealing with reading the *Shema*.[19]

But even for those who view Shmuel's dictum as a general prohibition of attentive listening to a woman's song or to her affectionate greeting, irrespective of *Shema*, this prohibition applies to the man's listening, not to the woman's singing(!)—the same way that he is forbidden to pleasurably gaze even at her little finger, but she is not required to cover her fingers.[20] R. Yosef adds that in certain circumstances the singing itself is provocative and thus prohibited.

In practice, even the disagreement as to the application of *kol be'ishah ervah* is limited. Since the sexually enticing nature of a woman's voice is not at issue, but only its role as an impediment to reading *Shema*, those who apply it to *Shema* expand its application, not limit it. They concur that for a man to focus on a woman's voice (or hair) constitutes a forbidden form of sexual excitement, regardless of whether or not the *Shema* is being recited. This stems directly from tractate *Berachot*: "In what context [did R. Yitzchak say 'An uncovered hand's-breadth...']? If regarding looking [at a woman], did not R. Sheshet say...? Rather, regarding his wife and reading *Shema*," i.e., an uncovered hand's-breadth of a woman is already subsumed under R. Sheshet's stricture against gazing even at their fingers; R. Yitzchak therefore establishes an *additional* prohibition, that of reading *Shema* while gazing even at one's wife (which is permitted at other times), but certainly does not permit gazing at other women. So, too, *kol be'ishah ervah* establishes a prohibition against reading the *Shema* while listening to any woman's voice (as does *se'ar be'ishah ervah* against looking at her hair), even the (singing) voice of one's wife, but does not permit listening to other women when not reading the *Shema*.[21] The *ervah* nature of a woman's voice being uncontested, it could hardly be otherwise.

R. Berman ignores this *sugya*. As a result, he errone-ously attributes to Franco-German *rishonim* the "restric-tion of Samuel's dictum to the recitation of *Shema*"—as if at other times listening to *kol be'ishah* is permitted. He notes that *Or Zarua*[22] is the only German *rishon* to deny the applicability of Shmuel's law to the recitation of *Shema* but remarks that "he fails to indicate what alternative applicability it might have."[23] In reality, the applicability of *kol be'ishah ervah* to general listening is crystal-clear. Rabbeinu Tam is explicit with regards to hair: "*Se'ar be'ishah ervah* applies to gazing at her but not to reading [*Shema*]";[24] the analogous application—prohibiting listening to her—adheres to Shmuel's dictum. This is directly stated in a view quoted in *Sefer haEshkol*:

> There is someone who says that it is permitted to read *Shema* even when one hears a woman's singing voice or sees her hair, if one doesn't intend to receive pleasure from it, and that *kol be'ishah* and *se'ar be'ishah* were not mentioned in the Gemara with regards to reading *Shema* but only to prohibit receiving pleasure from the voice and hair of an *ervah*.[25]

The prohibition against listening to *kol be'ishah* in general is explicit in *Ravad*, who understands the Gemara in *Berachot* as meaning "only regarding his wife" rather than "even regarding his wife," i.e., while reading *Shema* one may gaze at less than an uncovered hand's-breadth of one's wife because, being familiar with her, one is not distracted thereby from reading *Shema*, and because gazing at one's wife for pleasure is otherwise permitted. With another woman, by contrast, "it is forbidden to gaze at any part of her, even a little finger, and it is forbidden to listen even to her speaking voice..."[26] *Ravad*'s mention of R. Sheshet's "little finger" is proof, if any is needed, that regarding other women the prohibition is general and unconnected to reading the *Shema*. Unaccountably, R. Berman quotes other phrases from *Ravad* but not this one, and concludes: "it is not at all clear that *Ravad* would recognize the existence of a general bar to hearing the singing of a woman, other than in the case of recitation of *Shema*, in the absence of some special manifestation of warm friendship."[27] He overlooks the word "even" in the *Ravad*'s "even to her speaking voice," quotes the *Ravad*'s subsequent explanation that a woman's speaking voice is only forbidden "in issuing greetings or in responding to greetings...as in such case there is expression of warm friendship," and projects this qualification, which applies *only* to her speaking voice, onto her singing voice as well.

Ravad's position is, rather, precisely that of *Meiri*,[28] as opposed to R. Berman's attempt to portray *Meiri*'s as a lone opinion.

The conclusion from all of this is that the claim that the preponderance of *rishonim* profess no general prohibition to listening to *kol be'ishah* other than in the context of reading *Shema* or "of development of warm social relationships," is fundamentally mistaken, resulting from the author's having ignored the key discussion in *Berachot* and his failure to relate the *rishonim*'s opinions to their major source in the Gemara.

Still, parts of his discussion are illuminating, regarding the *achronim*, and his call for examining the practical parameters of *kol be'ishah* is well taken. We will

expand on one element that R. Berman mentions tan-
gentially, in the following chapter.

Notes

1. In *Rabbi Joseph H. Lookstein Memorial Volume*, Leo
    Landman, ed., Ktav, 1981, pp. 45–66. The essay has been
    widely circulated, and was the major source for a recent
    article on the subject in *Amudim*, the journal of the Re-
    ligious Kibbutz Movement in Israel.

2. *Ibid.*, p. 47.

3. This translation follows *Ravad*'s, *et al*, understanding. A
    second interpretation would be: "a woman's voice is
    [rabbinically equivalent to] *ervah*," literally, genitals. This
    refers to the prohibition in BT *Berachot* 25b and *Shabbat*
    103a, derived from *Devarim* 23:15, against reading
    Shema in the presence of uncovered genitals, including
    one's own.
       The difference between the two interpretations with re-
    gard to an exposed hand's-breadth of forbidden skin or
    hair, lies in circumstances where the uncovered part faces
    the reader but is not seen (and therefore there is no sexual
    excitement), such as at night or in the case of a blind pe r-
    son or one who averts or closes his eyes. The first view
    permits the reading of *Shema* while the second forbids:
    see *Biur Halachah* to *Orach Chayim* 75, *s.v. Be'makom
    shedarkah*. Adherents of the second view include *Sefer
    haEshkol* (Auerbach edition), pt. 1, ch. 7., *q.v.*; *Smag,
    aseh* 18; *Smak, mitzvah* 83; and *Rambam, Hilchot Kriat
    Shema* 3:17 as explained in *Bnei Tzion* (Lichtman), vol. 2,
    p. 87 (second column), contra *Nishmat Adam* 4:1.
       In the case of a woman's voice, the difference lies in
    circumstances where the voice is audible but no attention
    is paid to it. *Sefer haEshkol* forbids reading *Shema* in such
    a case, as does *Yeraim haShalem*, sec. 392, who, however,

relies on *eit la'asot laShem* to permit reading *Shema* even
when the singing of gentile women is audible. There is a
conceptual difficulty in including voice, which is invisible, in even a rabbinical extension of *"velo yeira'eh becha
ervat davar,"* "something *ervah* may not be *seen* in you"
(*Devarim* 23:15); see *Sefer Ravyah*, sec. 76.

4. *Hilchot Kri'at Shema* 3:17.

5. *Aseh* 16.

6. R. Yitzchak of Dampierre, quoted in *Sefer haAgudah*,
    Berachot, ch. 3.

7. Pt. 1, sec. 136.

8. Quoted in *Orchot Chayim, Hilchot Kri'at Shema*, par. 36,
    and *Piskei haRikanti*, no. 26; cf. *Ohel Moed*, vol. 1, p.
    49b. R. Tam explicitly excludes hair only, and makes no
    mention of voice, but there is no basis to include voice if
    hair is omitted.

9. BT *Berachot, loc. cit.*

10. *Mitzvah* 83.

11. *Piskei* and *Tosfot haRosh, Berachot* 24a.

12. *Orach Chayim* 75.

13. *Ibid*, par. 2-3. The *Shulchan Aruch* writes that "one
    should refrain" from hearing a woman's singing voice
    while reading *Shema*, i.e., he rules that voice constitutes
    no impediment but that nevertheless one should pay heed
    to the opposing opinion. Paying heed *lechatchilah* to a
    minority opinion is standard halachic practice; R. Berman
    (p. 57) sets up an artificial contradiction within the *Shul-
    chan Aruch* on this matter.

14. Quoted in *R. Yonah* to *Berachot* 25a, *s.v. Ervah*. His is also probably the opinion quoted in *Sefer haEshol*, see note 24, below.

15. Quoted by *Ravyah* and others.

16. *Loc. cit.*

17. Quoted in *Sefer haHashlamah* to *Berachot* 24a, and *Sefer haMe'orot* and *Chiddushei haRashba* to 25a.

18. *Ibid.*

19. *Kol be'ishah ervah* may not be applied by R. Yosef to the singing by groups of men and women also for the purely technical reason of "*trei kali lo mishtamei*," "two voices are not heard at once" (*Rosh HaShanah* 27a); and see *Bnei Banim*, III, no. 25.2.

20. This is a common distinction. For instance, in *Berachot* 61a, "A man should not walk behind a woman in the road" (or: "in the marketplace"), because of impure thoughts, see Resp. *Radbaz*, II, no. 770, and *Shulchan Aruch*, *Even haEzer* 21:1; but there is no requirement that a woman avoid walking in front of a man as long as she does not try to be provocative, cf. *Avodah Zarah* 18a. Another activity prohibited to the man but not to the woman is counting coins from his hand to hers for the purpose of looking at her; see *Berachot*, *ad loc.* For other ramifications of this distinction see below, next chapter, and *Bnei Banim*, III, no. 26.1.

21. The one explicitly lenient opinion is that quoted by *Ravyah* in the name of "*yesh mefarshim*," that *kol be'ishah ervah* is: "because one usually looks at her when she is making music (*menagenet*)," i.e., there is no sexual excitement in her voice per se, but listening may lead to looking. It is not clear who is the source of this interpretation. R. Berman follows Aptowitzer in citing R. Hai

Gaon and *Ravad* as the source, but there is no proof for this; see *R. Yonah* and *Rashba loc. cit.* It may be that *yesh mefarshim* is solely concerned to explain how the invisible voice can be included with visible *ervah* as an impediment to *Shema*; see above, note 3.

22. *Loc. cit.*

23. P. 48.

24. *Piskei haRikanti*, sec. 26; cf. *Ri*, in *Sefer haAgudah, loc. cit.*

25. Pt. 1, ch. 7, p. 15. *Sefer haEshkol* disagrees with the view that they are not impediments to reading *Shema*.

26. Cited in note 17 above.

27. P. 52.

28. BT *Berachot* 24a.

Chapter Nine

HIRHUR AND COMMUNITY NORMS[1]

Is there halachic justification for the relatively open interaction between men and women in much of today's Orthodoxy, and if so, what is it?

First, some background:

Of the *halachot* relating to women, those concerning prayer and ritual relate to what women may or may not do. So too, questions of modesty in dress and the like deal with behavior by women themselves. The laws we will discuss today, on the other hand, are formulated as *male* imperatives. Some examples are: *Ve'al tarbeh sichah im ha'ishah*, "don't converse at length with a woman";[2] "a man should always greatly distance himself from women";[3] "one may not look at women who are forbidden to him"; and "it is forbidden to walk behind a woman in the market place."[5] In all of these, the Halacha places the onus of responsibility on the male, to refrain from improper thoughts or actions.

In practice, however, the burden in these areas has often been borne by the woman and not by the man. The reason for this is that the simplest way for men to avoid excessive conversation with women, closeness to women, and looking at women is to not have women around at all. This approach is one which keeps women in the home and out of the workplace and marketplace altogether or, at least, separates men from women in places of employment, transportation, in boards and committees of organizations and so forth. As we know, separate is not equal. Restricting women's *physical* place to the home or other private arenas effectively circumscribes her role and status in society.

All this may be true, but begs the question of Halacha. The danger is a real one: interaction between the sexes can lead to *hirhur* or impure thoughts by men about women, or to *kalut rosh* or improper levity. These are prohibitions firmly grounded in the Talmud[6] and *Shulchan Aruch*.[7] We are halachic Jews, and we should accept with faith and love even those disabilities and restrictions which the Halacha may place on us. Is there a halachic justification for the mingling of men and women in modern Orthodoxy?

Our brief discussion will begin with the Talmud, continue with early authorities, the *rishonim*, and conclude with later authorities, the *achronim*, up to close to our day.

In the Talmud we find a few cases of seemingly egregious behavior on the part of the Sages. In tractate *Ketuvot* (17a), R. Acha lifted a bride on his shoulders at her wedding and danced with her. In *Berachot* (20a) R. Gidel and R. Yochanan used to sit in front of the mikva while the women were leaving after *tevillah*, for reasons the Gemara explains. This behavior surprised their colleagues, who asked them about it, and the explanations they gave were similar: "To me, women are like white geese"[8] or, "to me she is like a wooden beam." In other words, they had no improper intentions or impure thoughts, and therefore no prohibition was involved.

Does this exemption—that if there are no impure thoughts there is no prohibition—apply to post-Talmudic times as well? The *rishonim* differ. *Sefer haChinuch* (188) states emphatically that this exemption does *not* apply: "[The rabbis of the Talmud] were like angels...they felt no evil feeling in anything, because of their great devotion to Torah and *mitzvot*. But we, nowadays, may not deviate in the slightest in all these matters, and we have to follow all of the regulations which keep us away [from women]." According to this, even the most saintly of persons today may not take special liberties in matters of *hirhur*.

However, at least three early authorities disagree with *Sefer haChinuch*. The first is Rav Hai Gaon, quoted by *Rabbeinu Yonah* in *Berachot* (25a). On the topic of *kol ishah* as an impediment to a man's reading the *Shema*, Rav Hai Gaon states that if a man can concentrate on his reading to an extent that he doesn't listen to the woman's voice and pays no attention to her, he may read the *Shema* while she is singing. According to this, based on subjective capabilities, the individual may permit to himself what would be prohibited to others. This is the same principle employed by R. Acha and the others in the Talmud.

The second authority is the Tosafist R. Yitzchak of Corbeil. In his *Sefer Mitzvot Katan* (30) he writes, simply, that looking at women is permitted "if they are to him like a wooden beam or white geese." As he does not limit this to the sages of the Talmud, it is clear that it applies to later generations as well.

The third *rishon* is R. Yom Tov ben Avraham, the *Ritva*. At the end of his commentary on tractate *Kiddushin*, *Ritva* writes:

> Everything depends on what a person recognizes in himself... If he recognizes that his impulses are overcome and under his control and he has no lust at all, he is permitted to look at and speak with an *ervah* [a woman forbidden to him] and inquire about a married woman's welfare. Such was the case with R. Yochanan who sat at the entrance to the mikva and was not afraid of evil impulses...and R. Ada ben Ahavah[9] who lifted a bride on his shoulders and danced with her and was not afraid of lustful thoughts, for the reason that we have stated.

R. Hai Gaon, *Sefer Mitzvot Katan,* and *Ritva* all disagree with the opinion of *Sefer haChinuch.* Still, we have not gotten very far. All we have established is that, according to a handful of *rishonim,* exceptionally pious individuals in every generation may take liberties that the average person may not. *Ritva* himself concludes: "It is not fitting to be lenient in this, except for a person of great piety who knows himself." *Poskim* are, understandably, leery of permitting people to rely on themselves in such matters.

A very different approach, however, was put forward by the 16th century authority, R. Shlomo Luria, the *Maharshal.* In his *Yam Shel Shlomoh* on *Kiddushin* (4:25), he prefaces[10] with the following remarks:

> Everything depends on what a person sees, and [if he] controls his impulses and can overcome them he is permitted to speak to and look at an *ervah* [a women forbidden to him] and inquire about her welfare. The *whole world* relies on this in using the services of, and speaking to, and looking at, women.

He subsequently quotes the *Ritva* in full. This is surprising, for the *Ritva* speaks of "a person of great piety who knows himself," whereas *Maharshal* speaks of the "whole world," that is to say, the entire community. The "whole world" is hardly in the category of persons of great piety who know themselves.

What *Maharshal* is saying is that the average *individual* may not rely upon himself to go beyond what others are permitted in these matters. When an entire *community* is accustomed to mingling with and speaking to women, on the other hand, their familiarity may be relied on to forestall sinful thoughts.

Maharshal's source for this distinction is the *Tosafot* in *Kiddushin* (82a). In the Gemara, "*hakol leshem shamayim*" ("all in the name of heaven") is used by R. Acha bar Ada to explain the special liberty he alone took in taking his betrothed granddaughter on his lap, but the *Tosafot* there write, "On [*hakol leshem shamayim*] we rely nowadays [in] that we make use of the services of women." The *Tosafot* employ this principle to justify widespread practices. This is precisely the equation employed by *Maharshal*.

It can be said that the "whole world" of modern Orthodoxy relies implicitly on this *Maharshal* in using the services of and speaking to and looking at women. I will note two additional *achronim* who follow the path forged by the *Maharshal*.

The first is the *Maharshal*'s student, R. Mordechai Yafeh, the author of the *Levush*. It is customary to add the phrase *shehasimchah beme'ono*, "in Whose abode is happiness" in *zimun* before *birkat hamazon* on the occasion of the festive meals following a wedding. The 13th century *Sefer Chassidim* (393), however, specifically excludes meals "where women sit among the men, *hirhur* being present." Where there is mixed seating, then, *shehasimchah b'meono* may not be said.

The *Levush*, however, writes on this issue in his *Min-hagim* that "We do not take care [about avoiding mixed seating] because nowadays women are very common among men, and there are relatively few sinful thoughts [about them] because they seem to us like 'white geese' due to the frequency of their being among us..."[11] This is identical to the approach found in the *Yam Shel Shlo-moh*,[12] and indeed, *shehasimchah beme'ono* is today universally recited even in communities where there is mixed seating at *sheva berachot*.

The second and relatively recent authority is the late 19th century author of the *Aruch haShulchan*, R. Yechiel Michal Epstein. We have already mentioned that there are things that prevent a man from reciting the *Shema*; one of these is the uncovered hair of a married woman. Nevertheless, the *Aruch haShulchan* (*Orach Chayim* 75:7) writes:

> For many years Jewish women have been flagrant in this sin and go bareheaded...married women go about with [uncovered] hair like girls—woe to us that this has oc-curred in our day. Nonetheless, by law it would appear that we are allowed to pray and say blessings facing their uncovered heads, since the majority go about this way and it has become like [normally] uncovered parts of her body...

That is to say, although it remains forbidden for mar-ried women to go bareheaded in public, since they do so anyway, their hair is no longer an impediment to a man's reading the *Shema*. The reason for this is that since men are used to seeing it, women's hair is no longer a cause of *hirhur*—precisely the approach of the *Maharshal*.

We have seen, then, that there exists a trend—not a dominant trend, but a trend—within halachic thought that in interactions between the sexes that might ordinarily lead to *hirhur*, frequency and familiarity of contact can be a mitigating factor, and that a community can legitimately rely on this "in using the services of, and speaking to, and looking at, women" to use the words of the *Maharshal*.[13]

And here we need some words of caution and qualification. First, the above applies only to mingling of men and women that is innocent *in and of itself*. No degree of frequency and familiarity can legitimize what is intrinsically or intentionally sexually stimulating. Examples are immodest or provocative dress, erotic performances and entertainment, and other pitfalls too numerous to be listed. A sin indulged in a thousand times remains a sin.

Second, frequency and familiarity of contact are a mitigating factor in certain *halachot*, but not in many others. The *Aruch haShulchan* waives the impediment of a married woman's uncovered hair as regards a man's reading *Shema*, but clearly forbids the act of going bareheaded itself. There are people who misread the *Aruch haShulchan* as if he permits women going bareheaded. Their mistake lies in confusing the requirement for a married woman to cover her hair in public with the need to avoid causing *hirhur*. In fact, the two are separate *halachot* stemming from two completely separate Talmudic discussions.[14]

We have mentioned accepting with love and faith the restraints that Halacha may place on us. Head-covering for married women is an example of this.

Third, there is no halachic imperative to introduce mingling of the sexes where it does not already exist. What we have said here is a *justification* of community practices, not an agenda. It is much easier to legitimize existing practice than to justify new ones. To do the latter, we would have to take into account the approaches of far more *achronim* than just the *Yam Shel Shelomoh*, the *Levush*, and the *Aruch haShulchan*.

In this, as in other areas, our communities need rabbinic guidance which is both authoritative *and* sensitive.[15]

I would like to close with a famous Talmudic anecdote that bears on our topic. In tractate *Eiruvin* (53b): "R. Yosi the Galilean was walking along the road, when he met Beruria. He asked her 'Which is the road we take to Lod?' She responded, 'Stupid Galilean! Don't the Sages say not to converse at length with a woman? You should have said, "Which way to Lod?"'"

On the face of it, Beruria, the greatest woman Torah scholar in the Talmud, seems to have internalized the injunction against men speaking to women in a somewhat extreme fashion. But I think that's not what she meant. Take the following example: You are walking along the street in the nineteen-sixties and you suddenly meet Rabbi Soloveitchik. You say to him, "Oh, Rabbi Soloveichik, tell me, which way to the subway?"

Which way to the subway!? You've just met a *gadol hador*, and the only thing you have to say is, which way to the subway? Maybe ask him something regarding Torah?

That is what Beruria meant. She was a famous scholar, one who used to learn 300 *halachot* from 300 sources,[16] and all R. Yosi had to say to her was to ask directions? Well then, she said, if you're going to be that extreme in not speaking to women, follow that approach to its logical conclusion. Don't say, "Which is the road we take to Lod?" in eight words, when you can say "Which way to Lod?" in four!

It is my hope that a dialogue be established between rabbis and learned women, a dialogue that will consist more of Torah than of giving directions. And, may we all look forward next year to a conference not on "Feminism and Orthodoxy," but on Feminism *in* Orthodoxy.

Notes

1. This address was delivered to a conference plenum of 2,000 women in February 1998.

2. *Avot* 1:5.

3. *Tur* and *Shulchan Aruch, Even haEzer* 21:1.

4. See BT *Shabbat* 64a–b.

5. Tur and *Shulchan Aruch*, Ibid., from BT *Berachot* 61a and *Avot deRabi Natan* 2:2.

6. BT *Ketuvot* 46a, *et al*; *Avot* 3:12.

7. *Loc. cit.*

8. Perhaps this simile was used because it was common to bring geese from market over one's shoulders.

9. Our texts in *Ketuvot* 17a read: R. Acha.

10. On the question of the authorship of the introductions in *Yam Shel Shlomoh*, see *Bnei Banim*, I, p. 35 (note), and II, p. 233.

11. No. 36, at the end of *Levush haTechelet vehaChur* (*Orach Chayim*).

12. *Maharshal* himself, however, in *Yam Shel Shelomoh* to *Ketuvot* 1:20, approvingly quotes *Sefer Chassidim* on not saying *shehasimchah beme'ono* where there is mixed seating. Presumably, the merry nature of a wedding feast makes it more problematic, in this view, than ordinary occasions. Also, *Maharshal* writes that the custom "in my country...in most places" was that men and women at *sheva berachot* feasted in separate rooms—as opposed to the custom reported by the *Levush*. Therefore, there was no call for him to justify mixing of the sexes in this regard. For an extensive discussion on mixed seating at weddings and other occasions see *Bnei Banim*, I, no. 35, and *Otzar Haposkim* (vol. 17) to *Even haEzer* 62:13, pp. 106–7. It should be noted that *Aruch haShulchan* in *Even haEzer* 62 omits mention of *Sefer Chassidim* altogether.

13. Mixing of the sexes at weddings, social gatherings, and even Torah lectures was also characteristic of the strictly Orthodox Germanic-Dutch communities. Most of these communities were destroyed in the Holocaust, but their remnants in various places in Europe and America largely continue the practice. I am grateful to Rabbi F. J. Lewis of Amsterdam for this observation.

14. BT *Ketuvot* 72a and *Berachot* 24a. For an extensive discussion of the parameters of women's hair covering, see *Bnei Banim*, III, nos. 21-24.

15. A recent pronouncement by a group of New York area rabbis prohibiting a long list of activities by women was not authoritative, in that it included activities such as women's *Megillah* readings that are clearly not forbidden by Halacha; see chapter seven above and *Bnei Banim*, II, no. 10, pp. 39–40. Nor was this pronouncement sensitive, in my opinion, as the way to maintain influence is not through blanket prohibitions, but by seeking out points of agreement. Blanket prohibitions lead to a complete

breakdown in communication, and that is what resulted in this case.

On the question of other innovations in women's rituals see *Ibid.*, pp. 42–44, and R. Aryeh and R. Dov Frimer's article in *Tradition* 32:2 (Winter 1998) pp. 5–118.

16. BT *Pesachim* 63b.

Chapter Ten

CONVERTING CHILDREN IN NON-OBSERVANT FAMILIES

Intermarriage and Conversion: a Halakhic Solution[1] by Rabbi J. Simcha Cohen attempts to solve a problem facing many congregational rabbis: conversion of non-Jewish children adopted by non-observant Jewish members of the synagogue or, even, children born to couples where the husband is Jewish but not the wife.

In both cases, observance of *mitzvot* by the convert, normally a *sine qua non* for conversion, cannot be expected. With regard to minors under the age of bar or *bat mitzvah*, however, *kabbalat mitzvot* is not required for conversion.[2]

The problem lies in the fact that conversion requires consent. A minor below *bar mitzvah* or *bat mitzvah* is legally incompetent and cannot testify as to his or her own consent; indeed, legally he or she is not considered present in the courtroom at all. The Talmud removes this impediment by having the *beit din* accept conversion on the child's behalf (*al da'at beit din*), under the principle "one can act on behalf of a person to his advantage [even] in his absence,"[3] the premise being that were he present and competent he would concur. This assumes that it is to the child's benefit to become Jewish. Modern authorities,[4] however, raise serious doubts that this applies if he will be raised as a non-observant Jew. In that case, it may be to his detriment to convert, bringing into play the other half of the above-mentioned principle, "...but one cannot act on his behalf to his disadvantage in his absence." The conversion, therefore, would be invalid.

If, however, it could be determined that the child wished to convert regardless of the consequences, the conversion would be valid even if detrimental. The Talmud cites the case of "a proselyte whose sons and daughters were converted with him, so they are satisfied with what their father does."[5] In this case, *da'at beit din* and the question of benefit or detriment are bypassed and the minors are assumed to consent because they wish to do what their father does. This is the opinion of the *Tur* and *Shulchan Aruch*:[6]

> [Regarding] a minor Gentile, if he has a father [his father] can convert him. And if he has no father and he comes to convert or his mother brings him to convert, *beit din* converts him, because it is to his advantage and one acts to a person's advantage in his absence. A minor, whether his father converted him or *beit din* converted him, can renounce his conversion when he reaches [the age of] majority.[7]

Obviously, the non-Jewish, or even the Jewish, adoptive father cannot convert the child all by himself; he too, needs a *beit din* to perform the conversion ceremony. The point of listing him as an independent agent is that in this case the child's consent is assumed since "he is satisfied with what his father does," and future "benefit" need not be established.

This analysis parallels that of R. Cohen, who, however, takes matters further and writes, not only that presumption of benefit is not legally requisite in the case of a father converting his children, but that "any questions as to whether [the conversion] is an advantage or a liability are immaterial to the conversion process."[8] "...Concern for observance is totally extraneous to the issue."[9] "...Jewish fathers of such marriages who bring their infant children to *beit din* for conversion purposes *should not* be rejected"[10] (emphasis mine). In this the author confuses *lechatchilah* with *bedi'eved*, discounts the independent role of *beit din*, and overlooks various *rishonim*.

Except for the case of a Gentile who repeatedly demonstrates his sincere desire to convert[11]—inapplicable in the case of a minor—*beit din* is under no obligation to convert anyone.[12] Moreover, only a wicked *beit din* would convert someone to that person's detriment, whether or not they technically have the power to do so. As *Tosafot* write:

> That which the Gemara asks in *Ketuvot* "have we not already learned 'one can act on behalf of a person to his advantage in his absence'?" and answers "we might have thought that a Gentile prefers his life of license"—the reason is that if the conversion were to his detriment, *beit din* should not have intervened to involve itself in a matter which is to his detriment.[13]

Thus, the question of the benefit to the child remains, not in invalidating a conversion performed on the initiative of the father, but in deciding whether to perform such a conversion in the first place.

R. Cohen invokes *Berachot* (10a) to support his contention that *beit din* should not concern itself with the question of whether or not the child will grow up observant. There, however, King Chizkiya had learned through prophecy that his as-yet-not conceived heir, Menashe, would be an idol-worshipper, and sought to refrain from procreation as a result. The prophet Yeshaya objected to relying on supernaturally-gained knowledge in order to abrogate a *mitzvah*, and told him, "Why do you inquire into the secrets of G-d? That which you are commanded you must do." This has no bearing on voluntarily accepting a convert in circumstances in which experience and common sense predict a difficult, if not a negative, outcome.[14] So too, the author's citation of *Rosh haShanah* (16b), "A person is judged only on the basis of his current actions" (and not on the basis of a possible future), refers to Heavenly punishment and is irrelevant.

Furthermore, *beit din* has an ongoing concern with the religious welfare of the child. This is implied in *Meiri*: "*Beit din* converts him on their initiative as if they are his parents, so that his affairs be given over to them to enter him into the covenant (*brit*) and into the holiness of belief."[15] Entering the covenant—circumcision for a male—is independent of age, but "holiness of belief" applies only to one capable of belief—the implication being that *beit din* looks after the child convert until he matures. Although *Meiri* continues, "*a fortiori*, if his father converted and his minor son converted with him, he [the son] enters the covenant and the holiness of belief through him," this merely indicates that the father automatically assumes the role of guardian that *bet din* would normally appoint for a minor who converted, as it would for any orphan, to bring the child into the holiness of belief as he matures.[16]

But even were we to accept R. Cohen's contention that the child's future as a nonobservant Jew is of no concern to *beit din*, the welfare of the community certainly is. Creating additional non-observant Jews is detrimental to the Orthodox community outside of Israel.[17] It weakens religious standards and influence, encourages religious deviance, and increases the likelihood of divinely-inspired afflictions from which all will suffer, observant and non-observant alike.[18]

A halachic solution that proposes blanket conversion of tens of thousands of adopted children and children of mixed marriages without regard to observance of the *mitzvot*,[19] cannot be sustained.[20]

Notes

1. Ktav, 1987.

2. *Shitah Mekubetzet* to *Ketuvot* 11a, p. 104 (second column), in the name of Ritva and *Shitah Yeshanah*; *Dagul Meirvavah*, *Yoreh De'ah* 268:3.

3. BT *Ketuvot* 11a.

4. Resp. *Sridei Esh*, II, nos. 95–6; Resp. *Minchat Yitzchak*, III, no. 99. But see Resp. *Mahardach*, *bayit* 12, sec. 9, who defines *zechut* as pragmatic rather than spiritual benefit.

5. BT *Ketuvot* 11a. According to *Ritva* and *Meiri*, only when the Gentile father converts together with his children does the presumption "they are satisfied with what their father does" apply, but not if he remains a Gentile. However, it seems likely that if he is already Jewish, his children would also wish to be Jewish like their father, even though he does not undergo the conversion procedures with them.

6. *Yoreh De'ah* 268.

7. *Ibid.*, par. 7. On the approaches of the *rishonim* in general and the difference between the father and mother in converting children, see *Bnei Banim*, II, no. 36, pp. 136–9.

8. P. 12.

9. P. 13.

10. P. 21.

11. *Tosafot, Yevamot* 109b, *s. v. Ra'ah tachat ra'ah.*

12. *Beit din*'s obligation to convert commences only after a decision is reached to accept the candidate; see *Bnei Banim, ibid.,* p. 141.

13. *Tosafot, Sanhedrin* 68b, *s.v. Katan.* While *Tosafot* in *Sanhedrin* and in *Ketuvot* 11a differ in their analyses of the conversion process of a minor, they would not disagree on this point. R. Cohen notes the *Tosafot* in *Sanhedrin* in passing, on p. 50, but misses its significance.

14. See BT *Bava Batra* 70b, "It would be fitting that we decree a ban on procreation" during periods of severe anti-religious repression. See also *Yam Shel Shlomoh, Yevamot* 6:44, "A woman is allowed to drink a contraceptive potion if she...is afraid of unworthy offspring."

15. BT *Ketuvot* 11a.

16. According to Halacha, a convert lacks lineage as if he or she had no parents, even if the natural parents converted at the same time.

17. R. Moshe Feinstein in Resp. *Igrot Moshe, Yoreh De'ah,* I, no. 157, writes: "I don't understand the thinking of those rabbis who err in this. Even according to their reasoning, what benefit do they bring to *klal Yisrael* by ad-

mitting converts of this sort? Certainly it is not desirous to G-d and to Israel," i.e., even according to the opinion of rabbis who (mistakenly) think that conversion of an adult without his commitment to observe the *mitzvot* is valid, still, what benefit accrues from it? This equally applies to conversion of minors: even if construed as valid, if the children grow up non-observant such conversions are not to the benefit of the Jewish community. R. Cohen, on pp. 26–7, misconstrues this responsum. It should be noted that if conversions of minors are detrimental to others, the conversions may be invalid; see *Sma, Choshen Mishpat* 105:1.

This discussion applies only to North America and other countries outside of Israel. The situation in Israel is very different: at issue are a small number of adopted children a year, in families where both spouses are usually Jewish, in a society where intermarriage is not yet a problem. In fact, the danger is more that unconverted children will assimilate into Israeli society, leading to unnoticed and inadvertent intermarriages. The non-separation of Synagogue and State also makes it important to reduce religious/secular tensions if halachically possible. In such circumstances, it may be to the benefit of the Israeli community to convert children adopted in non-observant families.

18. *Rashi, Niddah* 13b, *s.v. Kesapachat*: "Proselytes are as damaging to Israel as a sore on the skin, because they are poorly versed in the commandments and bring Divine punishment," i.e., although they sin through ignorance and not though premeditation, the nation of Israel is punished nevertheless.

19. *Igrot Moshe, Even haEzer*, IV, no. 26, approves the conversion of minors if they are registered in a yeshiva day school. I have suggested that the conversion be made conditional on their remaining in day school and remain-

ing members of an Orthodox synagogue until *bar* or *bat mitzvah*, only at which time should a permanent certificate of conversion be issued. See *Bnei Banim, ibid.*, pp. 142–3.

20. R. Cohen writes, in response to criticism that his publication in English may cause the public to err, "Such assertions normally should be anticipated from medieval theologians. In that era, the masses were ignorant and to be shielded from potential error" (p. 39). "Medieval" is hardly a term of opprobrium in the history of Jewish scholarship, and the male population in medieval Europe, and certainly the rabbinate, was more Jewishly learned than it is today. On Jewish education in the Middle Ages, see *Encyclopaedia Judaica*, vol. 6, *s.v.* Education, pp. 407–11.

R. Cohen further writes, "Halachah should not be the esoteric province of a small number of scholars. All Jews must be aware of its principles and methodology... Thus, the purpose of publishing this responsum (and others) in English is not solely to engage the concern of halakhic scholars. It is to make the public aware of a halakhic approach to a variety of issues affecting the community at large. It is a form of public Torah learning... This, of course, does not preclude the publication of the material in Hebrew." (p. 36). Had the author indeed published his proposal in Hebrew to enable its review by competent halachic authorities, or, if in English, in a scholarly journal where it could be responded to in subsequent issues, there might have been no quarrel with his procedure, but to publish it solely in a popular English format appears as an attempt to circumvent the accepted halachic process.

Chapter Eleven

KILLING CAPTURED TERRORISTS

It can easily be established that the killing of non-Jews is prohibited,[1] either *mide'oraita*[2] or *miderabbanan*,[3] regardless of whether it is done directly or indirectly (*grama*).[4] Even idol-worshipers violating Noachide prohibitions may not be killed without prior trial.[5] A non-Jew who merely wounds a Jew is not subject to the death penalty.[6] Nor even can a murderer, when in custody and posing no immediate threat, be dealt with as a *rodef*.[7]

All this, however, applies to gentiles in peacetime. Regarding war, the Halacha is radically different. This is succinctly expressed in *masechet Soferim* (16:10): "Kill [even] the best from among the nations during wartime."[8]

A more halachic formulation can be found in *Rambam* in *Hilchot Rotzeach* (4:11): "Non-Jews with whom we are not at war (*she'ein beineinu ubeinam milchamah*)...one may not cause their deaths." His language is somewhat different in *Hilchot Avodah Zarah* (10:1): "...to physically destroy him [the non-Jew] or to push him into a pit is forbidden, because he is not warring with us (*she'eino oseh imanu milchamah*)." Ergo, when at war with them both direct and indirect homicide are permitted.

The difference in language between the two *halachot* ("at war" versus "warring") as well as *Rambam*'s use of the singular ("because *he* is not warring") in *Hilchot Avodah Zarah* imply, in my opinion, that even in the absence of general hostilities and a state of war between Jews and Arabs, an individual terrorist who attempts to kill Jews for nationalistic reasons is subject to the *halachot* of war.[9] And in war, according to Torah law, there is no difference between before and after capture.[10]

There are, however, two additional considerations. The first is *dina de'malchuta dina*, "the law of the kingdom is the law."[11] Today's duly constituted regime in Israel prohibits slaying terrorist prisoners, or any others.

The second is *chilul haShem*, profanation of the Divine Name, which is relevant even vis-a-vis non-Jews and even during wartime. During the conquest of Canaan, "Israel did not smite them [the Gibeonites], because the elders of the community had sworn to them" (Joshua 9:18). The Gibeonites had concealed their Canaanite identity and posed as residents of a distant country, and thus deceitfully obtained a non-aggression pact. The oath sworn to them was therefore invalid; nevertheless, "because of *kedushat haShem*"[12] they were not killed, so that the nations would not say that Israel violated its oath. *Chilul haShem* would have resulted had other peoples—no friends of Israel—believed that Israel had sworn falsely, not knowing that the oath was, in fact, null and void.

There are, in addition, circumstances which result in *chilul haShem* even when Israel's actions are legal according to Halacha, and the nations know that they are halachically sanctioned, but instead cast aspersions on

the Halacha itself. This emerges from the Jerusalem
Talmud (*Bava Kama* 4:3):

> The government once sent two officials to learn Torah
> from Rabban Gamliel, and they learned Scripture,
> Mishna, Talmud, *halachot* and *aggadot* from him.[13] Fi-
> nally they told him, "Your entire Torah is becoming and
> praiseworthy, except for these two things: you say a
> Jewess should not assist a Canaanite woman in childbirth
> but a Canaanite women can assist a Jewess in childbirth,
> [and also] a Jewess should not nurse the baby of a Ca-
> naanite woman but a Canaanite woman can nurse the
> baby of a Jewess in her presence; theft from Jews is for-
> bidden but from Canaanites [it] is permitted." That same
> hour, Rabban Gamliel decreed that theft from Canaanites
> is to be forbidden because of *chillul haShem*.

R. Gamliel held a minority opinion found in the Talmud that theft from non-Jews is permitted by the Torah,[14] yet he forbade it lest the gentiles think that Israel's
behavior was not "becoming and praiseworthy" but
despicable. Similarly, *Smag* writes, "I expounded to the
exiled communities of Israel that those who lie to the
gentiles and steal from them are in the category of
mechalelei haShem, since the gentiles will say Israel has
no Torah," i.e., if Israel behaves in such fashion,
non-Jews will say its religion is defective.[15]

The above applies only to Jewish behavior toward
non-Jews; regarding *halachot* between Jew and Jew, let
alone between Jew and G-d, gentile opinion has little
standing. The concept of *chilul haShem* requires de-
lineation even in relations with non-Jews—are we to
forbid everything non-Jews dislike? Still, exaggerations
cannot deter us from rejecting acts which are clearly

repugnant to the great majority of Jews and gentiles alike.

Responsa *Chavot Yair*[16] discusses the case of a Jewish thief hanged by the non-Jewish authorities who left his corpse on the gallows, the question being whether the community was obligated to ransom the corpse for burial since it continually reminded the gentiles of his thefts and thus constituted *chilul haShem*. He answered, "Even though there is *chilul haShem* in that the gentiles accuse Judaism in general because of this [thief], such are only the words of the rabble but not of the learned among them nor of their government. Don't they find thieves among them as well, to the thousands?"[17] When, however, an act is not widespread among the Gentiles, and their governments and scholars are unanimous in its condemnation, *chilul haShem* is certainly applicable, and such is the case regarding the killing of captured and bound terrorists.[18]

Postscript

In the spring of 1993, an Arab with a hand grenade hidden in his clothing was apprehended by residents of a Jewish village south of Hebron. He was tied hand and foot, and the army was called. In the meantime, a resident of a neighboring settlement happened on the scene. Informed that the terrorist, who was lying on the ground, had had a grenade, he immediately shot and killed him. He was arrested and charged with murder.

The incident evoked wide coverage in the Israeli and foreign media and heated discussion within the Jewish population of Judea and Samaria. A rabbi of an established settlement in the Shomron addressed a related question in an issue of *Gilyon Rabbanei Yesh"a*. He wrote: "From the perspective of *din*, this stabber is liable to death even when he has not killed anyone, although a Jewish *beit din* does not execute him as explained in *Rambam Hilchot Melachim* (10:6). However, *bedi'eved* if someone kills him, he is not punished for doing so."

I wrote to him that his answer was too short in view of the importance of the question, and that the aspect of *chilul haShem* should have been considered.

He wrote in reply that "the categories of *chilul haShem* are detailed in [*Rambam*] *Hilchot Yesodei haTorah* (5:10–11)...I do not see which of these two *halachot* has any connection to killing a bound terrorist."

I replied that *Hilchot Yesodei haTorah*, chapter 5, deals only with *chilul haShem* among Jews, but *chilul haShem* vis-a-vis non-Jews is mentioned elsewhere, particularly in *Hilchot Melachim* (6:5). I then discussed at length the law of a non-Jew who wounds a Jew, as well as the question of *chilul haShem*. This reply evoked no response. My suggestion to the editor of *Gilyon Rabbanei Yesh"a* that he print my reply, also evoked no response.

The following summer I wrote a detailed article, "The Prohibition of Killing Non-Jews and the Murder of a Bound Terrorist," and sent it to *Techumin*, a widely-read halachic annual of religious-nationalist views, to which I had previously contributed six articles.[19] Upon telephone inquiry some months later, I was told the article would not be printed because its topic was "delicate."

I then sent the article to a number of rabbis who served as advisors to *Techumin*. One responded as follows:

> ...The article is certainly worthy of publication, particu-
> larly as its conclusion is that even what is permitted by
> *din* is set aside because of *chilul haShem*.
>
> However, because of "the murmuring of the heretics,"[20]
> who are experts at taking things out of context, and a
> single phrase is enough for them to launch an unbridled
> attack on the Torah and the Rabbis—precisely during
> this period when the topic is very sensitive, it is desirable
> to refrain from any publicity [of the topic], to fulfill what
> is written "the wise will be silent at that time."[21]

To which I replied:

> I am surprised that you are fearful of the use that enemies
> of religion might make of it, but did not consider the goal
> of the article, [which is] to prevent forbidden acts of
> murder which damage us and Judaism. For is not your
> fear a mere apprehension, while the murders discussed—
> not only of bound captives—are already taking place,
> and every murder causes more damage than taking ten
> articles such as mine out of context.
>
> How can we not issue a halachic clarification which is
> needed to prevent current calamity, only because of fear
> of "lest they say," and repeat the mistake of R. Zecharia
> ben Avkulas?[22]

At question is not censorship *per se*. Total freedom of
expression regardless of consequences is halachically
untenable. Laws relating to non-Jews are particularly
problematic, and I myself have written against the public
airing of certain issues.[23] Nor can anyone deny the
vitriolic nature of attacks on religion, religious Jews and,
lately, religious residents of Judea and Samaria, found in
parts of the Israeli press and media—attacks rare in
America, where religion is usually a unifying rather than
a divisive force.

There is, however, a basic difference between airing theoretical halachic questions and between clarifying actual, contemporary problems. Through the centuries, the idea of Jews murdering non-Jews was divorced from reality,[24] and public discussion of it could only result in gratuitous ferment, if not disastrous consequences. Today, however, it is a burning issue that will not go away.

Additional Postscript

A letter I subsequently wrote protesting *Techumin*'s "missing an important opportunity to clarify a clear and pressing issue, *halachah lema'aseh*," appeared in the settlers' journal *Nekudah* two weeks before the Purim 1994 killing of Arabs in the mosque on top of the Machpela cave in Hebron. The article itself eventually appeared the following fall in the much less widely circulated *Shanah beShanah* (5755) annual of Heichal Shlomo, and subsequently in *Bnei Banim*, III, *ma'amar* 4. The abbreviated English version published here was rejected by the American Jewish Orthodox journal *Tradition*.

An eerie parallel to the above occurred the following year. In February 1995, a group of rabbis from *Irgun Rabbanei Yesh"a* wrote to forty prominent Israeli rabbis and *poskim* inquiring whether the Rabin government had the halachic status of *rodef* or *moser*. Only three acknowledged the question, and the only detailed answer, I was later told, was written by this writer.

While strongly advocating replacing this "bad government" with a better one, I argued, based on *Shavuot* 35b, that according to Halacha a Jewish government is within its rights in implementing policies even at the risk

of the lives of some of its citizens. The government and
its ministers, therefore, could not be considered *rodfim*.
The responsum concluded with an answer to "a question
you did not ask," (an allusion to the possibility of
political assassination), averring that "such a sin would
not bring salvation but would merely be revenge and
would endanger the many."

The group of rabbis did not make the responsum
public, and indeed kept the whole inquiry secret. I
eventually published the responsum in the rabbinical
journal *Keshot* that I edited. The issue containing the
responsum was at the printer at the time of the Rabin
assassination in November 1995. Shortly thereafter,
word of the original inquiry appeared in the Israeli press
and the group of rabbis became the subject of a police
investigation. Interviewed on the topic, a spokesman for
the group denied that any answers had been received to
their inquiry.[25]

Notes

1. *Rambam, Hilchot Avodah Zarah* 10:1, from *beraita* in
    BT *Avodah Zarah* 26b; Rashi to *Avodah Zarah* 13a, *s.v.*
    Ve'ein moridin, Tosafot to 10b, *s.v. Chad ketil*, and *Ha-
    gahot Ashri* to 54b; *haMeiri* to *Sanhedrin* 57a, *s.v. Ve-
    chein le'inyan shefichut damim, et al.*

2. See *Mechilta, Mishpatim*, ch. 4, *s.v. Vechi yazid ish*, end;
    Sanhedrin 59a, "*leika mid'am...*" and cf. *Chiddushei ha-
    Ran* to 57a, *s.v. kuti bekuti*; *Bet haMafte'ach* to *Rambam*
    (Frankel edition) *Hilchot Rotzeach* 4:11. For a complete
    discussion of the *Mechilta* and other sources, see my
    Resp. *Bnei Banim*, III, nos. 40–42.

3. *Yereim haShalem*, sec. 175; *Chiddushei Rabbeinu Yonah* to *Sanhedrin* 57a, *s.v. Hakutim*. See also *Taz, Yoreh De'ah* 158:1 regarding *Tosafot* to *Avodah Zarah* 26b, *s.v. V'Lo moridin*, but cf. *Tosfot Shantz, Tosfot Rabbeinu Elchanan* and *Tosfot haRosh, ad. loc.*

4. *Rambam, Hilchot Avodah Zarah, loc. cit.* and *Hilchot Rotzeach*, 4:11, and see *Orach Mishor* (in *Darchei Moshe haAroch*) to *Yoreh Deah* 158, and *Minchat Chinuch*, ch. 93; *Ri haZaken*, cited in *Temim Dayim*, ch. 203. Many *rishonim* explain that "*moridin*" in the *beraita* in *Avodah Zarah* 26b regarding Jewish heretics permits only indirect causation of death, and therefore "*ein moridin*," regarding non-Jews, would prohibit even indirect causation: see Resp. *haRosh* no. 32:4 and Resp. *Rivash* no. 137; *Chiddushei haRoeh* and *Piskei Riaz* to *Avodah Zarah* 26b. *Chiddushei haRitva* to *Makkot* 9a permits indirect causation of death (but not direct killing), and only of Gentiles who do not observe the seven Noachide commandments, e.g., pagans or barbarians. Cf. *Meiri* to *Bava Kama* 38a, *s.v. Shor shel Yisrael*; *Bnei Banim*, II, sec. 45.3.

5. *Hagahot Ashri* and *Tosafot, s.v. Eizehu ger toshav* to *Avodah Zarah* 64b. This may be *Rambam*'s intent in *Hilchot Avodah Zarah* 10:1, "One may not make a pact with idol worshippers...but they must renounce their creed or be killed... But to physically destroy him or to push him into a pit is forbidden." The former ("or be killed") applies when the judicial process is followed; the latter, in its absence.

    The requirement of judicial process illuminates a perplexing passage in I Samuel 15:23. Before killing Agag, Shmuel proclaimed, "As your sword made women bereft, so your mother will be bereft among women." What did this have to do with the commandment to exterminate Amalek? And see *Tanchuma* and *Tanchuma Yashan* to *Ki Teitzei*, "He judged him by the judicial procedures of the [other] nations, without [two] witnesses and without warning"—whereas to kill an Amalekite in accordance with Halacha, no judicial procedures are required at all. Cf. *Sefer haChinuch* (Chavel edition) ch. 558. The explanation is that after Agag was taken into custody, Shmuel executed him both to fulfill the commandment to obliterate Amalek and to punish him for his crimes. The first required no judicial procedures, but the second did; "As your sword..." constituted the *gezar din* for Agag's personal crimes.

6. *Rambam, Hilchot Melachim* 10:6, and *Meiri* to *Sanhedrin* 58b, s. v. *Kuti shehikah. Chiddushei haRan, ad loc.*, disagrees in theory but does not reject *Rambam*'s ruling.

7. "Pursuer," i.e., someone actively attempting to murder another, in which case the pursuer can be killed on the spot if necessary to save his victim, but only as long as the attempt is in progress: *Sanhedrin* 73a in Mishna and *beraita; Rambam* and *Kesef Mishneh, Hilchot Rotze'ach* 1:6, 12, *et al*. Also, a *rodef* may not be killed if it is possible to employ lesser means to thwart him. *Rambam* in 1:7 gives as examples "to cut off his hand or break his leg"— even though a broken leg can heal.

An exception to the rule that the laws of *rodef* apply only during the course of an attempted murder or rape but not afterwards, is the case of a Jewish recidivist informer (*moser*) who is killed under the presumption that he will inform again; see *Rambam, Hilchot Chovel uMeizik* 8:11 and *Shulchan Aruch, Choshen Mishpat* 388:11. Presumably, a hardened terrorist is no less inclined to kill Jews in the future. Nevertheless, even a recidivist may not be killed if he is incapable of carrying out his intentions; see *Yam Shel Shelomoh, Bava Kama* 10:50. This would apply to captured terrorists facing or already serving lengthy jail terms, but not if their early release is assured through prisoner exchanges or amnesty.

8. Cf. *Tosafot* to *Avodah Zarah* 26b, *s.v. Velo moridin*;
    Mechilta, Beshallach, ch. 1, *s.v. Vayikach shesh me'ot
    rechev*, quoted in *Rashi* to *Shemot* 14:7, and *Rabbeinu
    Bachayei, ad loc.* The statement in *masechet Soferim*
    comes in the context of other hyperbolic statements; see
    Bnei Banim, III, no. 40.

9. None of the commentators on *Rambam* remark on this,
    but it is clear to me that *Rambam* is alluding to the differ-
    ent categories of war he enumerates in *Hilchot Melachim*
    (5:14). "With whom we are not at war" refers to the ab-
    sence of a state of war between Israel and other nations,
    "*beineinu ubeinam*," i.e., the obligatory or voluntary wars
    listed in *Hilchot Melachim*. "Because he is not warring
    with us," on the other hand, refers to the absence of the
    third category mentioned there, that of rescuing Israel
    from attack ("*ezrat Yisrael miyad tzar haba aleihem*").
    The categories are very different. Obligatory and volun-
    tary wars are offensive conflicts, while rescuing Israel
    from attack is a defensive conflict. The former two are
    promulgated by the government, while the latter includes
    even spontaneous and local initiatives. Finally, a formal
    state of war can be obtained even in the absence of hos-
    tilities, while self-defense is solely in response to a mate-
    rial threat. The phrase *oseh milchamah* in *Rambam* con-
    sistently refers to actual combat; see *Hilchot Shabbat* 2:23
    and *Hilchot Melachim* 6:1, 4, 11.
        For halachic implications of these distinctions see *Bnei
    Banim*, II, *ma'amar* 3.

10. This is well known from *Devarim* 21:12–13, and see
    Rambam, Hilchot Melachim 6:4, *et al.* Nevertheless, the
    Geneva Convention signed by the State of Israel may be
    no less binding, because of *chilul haShem* than the oath
    made to the Gibeonites. In warfare there is no obligation

to disable an enemy rather than kill him; see *Knesset haGedolah* to *Choshen Mishpat, Hagahot haTur* 425:11.

11. *Rambam, Tur* and *Shulchan Aruch* rule that *dina demalchuta dina* applies to Jewish governments in the land of Israel as much as to non-Jewish ones abroad; see *Hilchot Gezeilah ve'Aveidah* 5:11; *Tur* and *Shulchan Aruch, Choshen Mishpat* 369:6. Concerning the opposing view of *Ran*, see Resp. *Chatam Sofer, Choshen Mishpat*, no. 44, *s.v. Ach haRan*; *Kitvei HaGri"a Henkin*, vol. 2., no. 96 (1), par. 6 and 10. Regulations limiting bloodshed are certainly among the legitimate concerns of a government. On the de facto legitimacy of a modern Israeli government, see *Bnei Banim*, III, no. 33.

12. BT *Gittin* 46a, i.e., *chilul haShem*; cf. *Rambam, Hilchot Melachim* 6:5.

13. See BT *Sanhedrin* 59a and *Chagigah* 13a regarding the prohibition of teaching Torah to Gentiles, and *Tosafot* to *Bava Kama* 38a, *s.v. Karu*. It is possible that the officials came in the guise of prospective converts and it was therefore permissible for R. Gamliel to teach them; see *Bnei Banim*, III, no. 14.

14. See BT *Bava Kama* 113a–b and *Bava Metzia* 111b.

15. *Lo Taaseh* 2.

16. No. 139.

17. The argument seems difficult in light of the above-mentioned *Smag*.

18. It need hardly be added that the same applies to the killing of Muslims at prayer.

19. In vols. 1, 2, 3, 4, 8, and 13.

20. BT *Berachot* 12a.

21. Amos 5:13.

22. BT *Gittin* 56a. Asked to give a halachic ruling which might have forestalled the outbreak of war with the Romans, R. Zecharia refused lest it be misconstrued. R. Yochanan considered him thereby responsible for the destruction of the Temple. See below, next chapter.

23. *Bnei Banim*, II, *ma'amar* 3; and see *Kitvei haGri"a Henkin*, vol. 2, no. 95(2). My article originally appeared in 1982 in *Nekudah*, the journal of the Jewish settlements in Judea, Samaria and Gaza, in protest against earlier articles there which highlighted *Rambam*'s stipulation, in *Hilchot Melachim* 6:1, that conquered peoples be subjugated, "lowly and degraded." I concluded that this did not apply to conquests resulting from wars of self-defense.

24. This state of affairs is implied at the beginning of *Shemot*. Moshe established his credentials as a rescuer by saving an Israelite from an Egyptian, an Israelite from another Israelite, and the daughters of Yitro from other gentiles. What about the fourth possibility in this typology, that of saving an Egyptian from an Israelite? Probably, under conditions of servitude in Egypt there was no opportunity to do so. On intervention to save a non-Jew from a Jew, see *Sefer Chassidim*, par. 1018.

25. In the Israeli newpaper *HaTzofeh*. For more on this affair, see *Keshot*, issue 7 (*Adar/Nisan* 5756), pp. 17–18; for the text of the Hebrew responsum, see issue 6 (*Cheshvan/Kislev* 5756), pp. 12–15 and *Bnei Banim*, III, no. 33. The text of the inquiry itself was not made public.

JEWISH THOUGHT

Chapter Twelve

WHY WAS THE SECOND TEMPLE DESTROYED?

Rabbi Zecharia's Mistake

To understand events in our time we first need to understand what caused the Exile which preceded them. The main Talmudic discussion of the destruction of the Second Temple is found in *Gittin* (55b). At first glance the account is perplexing, but upon reflection, it makes perfect sense; we will examine it in detail and see what the Gemara is trying to teach us.

> R. Yochanan said, what does the verse "Fortunate is the man who is always afraid, and one who stiffens his heart falls into calamity" (Proverbs 28:14) refer to? Jerusalem was destroyed because of Kamtza and Bar Kamtza... A certain man had a friend called Kamtza and an antagonist called Bar Kamtza.[1] He prepared a feast and instructed his servant to invite Kamtza, but the servant mistakenly invited Bar Kamtza. The man came to his feast and found Bar Kamtza sitting there. He said to him, "You're my enemy, so what are you doing here? Get up and get out!" Bar Kamtza said, "Since I already came, let me be and I'll pay you for what I eat and drink." The man said no. Bar Kamtza said, "I'll pay you half the entire cost of the feast." The man said no. Bar Kamtza said, "I'll pay

you the entire cost of the feast." The man said no, took his arm, stood him up and threw him out.

Bar Kamtza said, "Since there were rabbis there and they didn't protest [such behavior], evidently they approved of it. I'll go and slander them to the authorities." Bar Kamtza went and told the [representative of the] Emperor,[2] "The Jews have rebelled against you." He replied, "How can we be sure?" Bar Kamtza said, "Send a sacrifice in your name to the Temple, and see if they accept it."[3]

[The Emperor's representative] sent a corpulent cow via Bar Kamtza to bring to the Temple as a sacrifice. Along the way, Bar Kamtza blemished the animal in its upper lip—some say in a spot in its eye—which we consider a blemish but they [the Romans] don't. The rabbis advocated sacrificing it anyway for the sake of peace with the government, but R. Zecharia ben Avkulas told them, "People will say that blemished animals may be sacrificed on the altar." They advocated killing Bar Kamtza so he would not report back, but R. Zecharia ben Avkulas told them, "People will say that blemishing a sacrifice is punishable by death."

R. Yochanan said, "R. Zecharia ben Avkulas' forbearance (*anvatnuto*) destroyed our home and burnt our sanctuary and exiled us from our country."

Later we will dwell on R. Yochanan's conclusion that the destruction of the Temple was the result of one leader's miscalculations and not of sin, but first we have to understand R. Zecharia ben Avkulas. He was a judge of the Sanhedrin or some other high halachic authority, and he objected to sacrificing a blemished animal even as an emergency measure, lest people mistakenly think that normative Halacha permits it. He similarly objected to killing Bar Kamtza, lest people unaware that he was an informer conclude that blemishing a sacrifice is a capital crime. Their sacrifice having been rejected, the Romans concluded that the Jews had indeed rebelled, and the result was the destruction of the city and of the Temple and the beginning of the Exile.

How was it possible that R. Zecharia concerned himself with minutiae such as mistaken impressions in Halacha, when faced with the possibility of destruction of *klal Yisrael*?[4] Let people think and err as they may, nothing stands in the way of *pikuach nefesh* and certainly not before the fate of the entire nation!

Undoubtedly, R. Zecharia did not simply act on his own accord. He must have found some source for the idea that one should not foster a mistaken concept in Halacha even when faced with a threat to national existence. In my opinion, he derived this from the account of Pinchas and Moshe in *Bamidbar*, chapter 25 (1–9):

> Israel settled down in Shittim, and the people began to whore with Moabite women. They invited the people to the feasts of their gods, and the people ate and bowed to their gods. Israel attached itself to *Baal Peor*, and *haShem* was angry with Israel [and brought a plague on the people].
>
> *HaShem* said to Moshe, take all the leaders of the people, and, for *haShem*, hang the sinners in broad daylight so that *haShem*'s fury with Israel will be removed. Moshe instructed Israel's judges, "Everyone should kill those of his men who attached themselves to *Baal Peor*."
>
> Just then an Israelite man [Zimri] came, and together with the Midianite woman approached his fellows; they [the leaders] were crying near the entrance to the meeting tent. Pinchas the son of Elazar the son of Aharon the priest saw, and he arose from among the assemblage and took hold of a spear. He followed the Israelite into the

chamber and stabbed both of them, the Israelite and the woman through her stomach. The plague in Israel was halted; 24,000 had died in the plague.

Pinchas killed Zimri even though Zimri had not committed idolatry but had merely whored, based on the Halacha given orally at Sinai, *"habo'el aramit, kanaim pogim bo"* (zealots attack someone who [publicly] has relations with a non-Jewess), as explained in *Sanhedrin* (82a). The Gemara then asks why Pinchas decided the law by himself without consulting Moshe, since a student is normally forbidden to issue halachic rulings in the place of his teacher. The *amoraim* tie the discussion to the verse "Pinchas...saw": what did he see that others didn't, and why did he see fit to do the deed himself and not wait for Moshe? Three answers are given:

"Rav said: 'He saw what was happening and remembered a Halacha. He said to Moshe, "Grand-uncle, when you came down from Mt. Sinai, didn't you teach me that zealots attack someone who has relations with a non-Jewess?" Moshe replied, "Whoever reads the letter should be the emissary."'" Pinchas violated no prohibition because he first mentioned the Halacha to Moshe, who obliquely gave him the green light to act.

"Shmuel said, 'He saw that "there is no wisdom, understanding or counsel against *haShem*" [Proverbs 21:30]; when *chilul haShem* is present one does not defer to a teacher.'" Pinchas didn't need to consult Moshe because Zimri, head of the tribe of Shimon, had profaned the Name by publicly consorting with a Midianite woman.

"R. Yitzchak said in the name of R. Eliezer, 'He saw that an angel had come and was decimating the people.'"

In a life-and-death emergency one doesn't stand on protocol.

One may ask following Rav's explanation, when Moshe was reminded of the Halacha, why didn't *he* implement it himself? Moshe had himself been a zealot, "He killed the Egyptian and hid him in the sand" (*Shemot* 2:12). What is particularly problematic is that Moshe let Pinchas endanger himself, since Zimri's tribe would certainly seek to avenge the killing of their leader, as recounted in the Midrash.[5] The Talmud in *Sanhedrin* also notes that had Zimri overcome and killed Pinchas in self-defense he would not have been guilty of murder.

In fact, however, Moshe was ineligible to act on his own. The Talmud records the Halacha that "if he consults *beit din*, they do not instruct him" to kill the violator. The zealot must act on his own initiative without the sanction of the judiciary. Moshe was the head of the Sanhedrin and any act by him would be widely interpreted as embodying normative Halacha; therefore, he could not play the private role of a zealot and kill Zimri, nor could the other elders.

But the question remains: even if Moshe's killing Zimri might be misconstrued, even if people would mistakenly conclude that Zimri had been judicially liable to the death penalty and not merely to extra-legal punishment at the hands of a zealot, wasn't it a time of national crisis? The same question applies to Shmuel's and R. Yitzchak's explanations. Whatever the technical reason why Moshe did not kill Zimri—whether he forgot the Halacha about zealots or was otherwise precluded from carrying it out—why didn't he order him killed as an emergency measure to save Israel from destruction? Moshe knew the emergency existed: G-d had told him

"Take all the leaders of the people...so that *haShem*'s fury (*charon af*) with Israel be removed." G-d's fury and wrath (*cheimah*) precipitate destruction, as G-d subsequently said, "Pinchas...removed my wrath (*cheimati*) from the Israelites and I did not wipe them out in My wrath" (*Bamidbar* 25:11).

This, then, was a precedent for ruling that it is forbidden to foster a mistaken concept in Halacha even when national existence is threatened. Moshe did not take emergency measures against Zimri, even when faced with the danger of G-d wiping Israel out in a plague, and so too, R. Zecharia prevented the killing of Bar Kamtza. R. Yochanan's terminology is exact: "R. Zecharia ben Avkulas' forbearance (*anvatnuto*) destroyed our home..." *Anvatnut* is *anavah*, and *anavah* was the defining characteristic of Moshe, as noted in *Bamidbar* (12:3), "The person Moshe was very forbearing[6] (*anav me'od*)..." R. Zecharia learned from Moshe.

"That Refers to *Divrei Torah*"

If R. Zecharia based himself on Scripture, we have to understand why R. Yochanan accused him of causing the destruction of the Temple. But, in fact, that is exactly what R. Yochanan warned against in his introductory citation, "Fortunate is the man who is always afraid, and one who stiffens his heart falls into calamity." He meant: fortunate is one who is afraid lest he learned Torah improperly, lest he erred in his reasoning, lest he took insufficient care in reaching conclusions, and lest his teachings and rulings bring disaster.

This explains the first and only other discussion in the Talmud which quotes the verse "Fortunate is the man who is always afraid..." In *Berachot* (60a):

A student was walking behind R. Yishmael ben R. Yosi
in the Zion market. He sensed that the student was
frightened, and said to him "You are a sinner, as is written 'Sinners were frightened in Zion' (Isaiah 32:14)."
The student said, "Isn't it written, 'Fortunate is the man
who is always afraid'?" R. Yishmael replied, "That refers
to *divrei Torah.*"

Yehuda ben Natan was walking behind R. Himnuna.
Yehuda groaned, and R. Himnuna said to him, "A person
like you invites suffering, as is written, 'I feared a fear
and it caught up with me, and that which I dreaded will
occur'" [Job 3:25]. But isn't it written, "Fortunate is the
man who is always afraid"? That refers to *divrei Torah.*

Commenting in *Berachot* on "That refers to *divrei
Torah,*" *Rashi* takes it to mean that one should be afraid
of forgetting the Torah he learned, and therefore review
his studies constantly. But such is not the sense of the
rest of the verse "...one who stiffens his heart will fall
into calamity." From R. Yochanan's words in *Gittin*,
rather, it is clear that "That refers to *divrei Torah*" means
that one should be afraid of misunderstanding the Torah
and erring in his conclusions from it, as R. Zecharia ben
Avkulas erred in equating the case before him with the
situation facing Moshe. For he could have explained
Moshe's behavior differently. As for example, it seems
to me that when G-d told Moshe "Take all the leaders of
the people...so that *haShem*'s fury with Israel will be
removed," this was a promise that if he ordered the
idolaters killed this would be a sufficient response, and
he need do no more. R. Zecharia, at any rate, should
have considered that the precedent he found might not be
relevant to his day.

Moshe's not ordering Zimri's execution caused no damage, whereas R. Zecharia's taking no action against Bar Kamtza led to the Temple's destruction. The zealotry displayed by Pinchas saved Israel, but zealotry of a different sort destroyed *bayit sheini*, when the Zealots brought about civil war and the fall of Jerusalem. "Fortunate is the man who is always afraid..."—that refers to *divrei Torah*!

Two Types of Leadership

The lesson that a leader must consider the possibility of error and not endanger Israel on the strength of his understanding alone of Torah, is also the point of the Jerusalem Talmud in *Berachot* (9:5) and *Sotah* (5:5). In both places, the account of the death of R. Akiva *al kiddush haShem* is immediately followed by his exposition of *Devarim* 6:13: "R. Akiva said, 'You shall fear *haShem*, your G-d' (*et haShem elokecha tira*)—fear Him and His Torah (*oto ve'et torato*)." This is commonly taken to mean the same as the version quoted by the Babylonian Talmud in *Pesachim* (22a), "R. Akiva said...fear Torah scholars as well" (*lerabot talmidei chachamim*), but the wordings of the two Talmuds are very different. Rather, R. Akiva had declared, based on his studies, that Bar Kochva was the Messiah, and he was therefore partly to blame for the revolt that cost hundreds of thousands of Jewish lives. Before his death at the hands of the Romans, he acknowledged that he should have been more afraid of the possibility of error,[7] for a scholar must fear the Torah as he fears G-d. "Fortunate is the man who is always afraid..."—that refers to *divrei Torah*!

This explanation also illuminates a discussion in *Rosh HaShanah* (25a). The Talmud discusses the authority of a leader, and comments on the Torah's not having recorded the names of the elders who were appointed to help Moshe, in *Bamidar* chapter 11. "Our rabbis taught, why weren't their names listed? So that no one [today] will say: 'Is X like Moshe or Aharon?' 'Is Y like Nadav or Avihu?' 'Is Z like Eldad or Meidad?'" i.e., even if contemporary leaders cannot compare with Moshe, Aharon, and so forth, perhaps they can compare with the elders whose names are not mentioned but who nevertheless had the Divine spirit rest on them. The Talmud continues:

> It is stated, "Shmuel said to the people, '*HaShem*, who made Moshe and Aharon,'" and it is [also] stated, "*HaShem* sent Yerubaal, Bedan, Yiftach and Shmuel" (I Samuel 12:6,11). Yerubaal is Gideon... Bedan is Shimshon... It is [also] stated, "Moshe and Aharon among His priests, and Shmuel among those who call His Name" (Psalms 99: 6).
>
> [The fact that] Scripture equated three lightweights with three heavyweights [comes] to teach you: Yerubaal in his generation is like Moshe in his generation; Bedan in his generation is like Aharon in his generation; Yiftach in his generation is like Shmuel in his generation.

If someone in Gideon's time questioned his authority, he could be answered "Yerubaal in his generation is like Moshe in his generation." Similarly, in Shimshon's time one could say "Bedan in his generation is like Aharon in his generation." In Yiftach's time, on the other hand, Shmuel had not yet been born. What, then, is the point of "Yiftach in his generation is like Shmuel in his generation"?

The point is that there are two types of leadership. A leader may need to do what other leaders already did before him, and people should not object that the others had the stature to do so but he doesn't; concerning him the Sages said, "Yerubaal in his generation is like Moshe in his generation." But sometimes a leader needs to do what has not been done before, in circumstances for which there is no clear precedent. He cannot always base himself on the past. The Sages said, "Yiftach in his generation is like Shmuel in his generation," for even if it seems that he lacks the authority to innovate, future leaders will arise and endorse his actions.

R. Zecharia ben Avkulas found in the Torah a situation he considered parallel to his own, and based himself wholly on the past. For that reason R. Yochanan mourned that his lack of leadership[8] "destroyed our home and burnt our sanctuary and exiled us from our country."

Baseless Hatred

Whatever we make of R. Zecharia, his rulings were not in the category of sins, and certainly not sins punishable by destruction and exile. What, then, is the meaning of R. Yochanan's statement, which attributed the *churban* to the mistakes of one leader and not to sin?

In fact, the other key Talmudic explanation of the destruction of the Second Temple also doesn't attribute it to sin. We read in *Yoma* (9b):

> Why was the First Temple destroyed? Because of three things which were present: idolatry, illicit sexual relations and murder... But the Second Temple, [when] they were occupied with Torah, *mitzvot*, and acts of kindness

(*gemilut chassadim*)—why was it destroyed? Because of baseless hatred which was present. To teach you, that baseless hatred (*sinat chinam*) is equal to the three sins: idolatry, illicit sexual relations, and murder.

The term "baseless hatred" requires clarification. Hatred is prohibited in *Vayikra* (19:17), "You shall not hate your fellow in your heart," but this is not the *sinat chinam* the Gemara is referring to. The verse refers to hatred "in your heart," i.e., surreptitious or masked enmity, whereas to illustrate *sinat chinam* the Gemara in *Yoma* quotes Ezekiel (21:7), "Groups [armed] with the sword were with my people," and explains, "These are men who eat and drink, and stab each other with verbal swords," out loud and in public.

In *Vayikra* 19:18 the Torah commands, "Love your fellow as you do yourself," and R. Akiva considered this "a basic principle of the Torah."[9] But violating this principle and refraining from neighborly acts of kindness and brotherhood is also not what the Gemara is referring to, for we already read that during the second Temple period people were occupied with "Torah, *mitzvot*, and acts of kindness."

Underlying these difficulties is a fundamental problem. If *sinat chinam* refers to sins, where is there warning in Scripture of any punishment for it, let alone destruction of the Temple and exile? G-d does not punish without prior admonition. Nor is *sinat chinam* listed among the sins which incur exile, as recorded in *Avot* (5:9): "Exile is brought to the world by idolatry, by illicit sexual relations, by murder, and by [non-observance of] the Sabbatical year." Similarly, in *Shabbat* (33a) the Sages said, "Because of the sins of idolatry, illicit sexual relations, (and) murder, (and) the abrogation of the Sabbatical, and Jubilee years, exile is brought to the world and they are exiled," and also "because of the sin of murder the Temple is destroyed," and they cited verses from the Torah which warned of the consequences of each of these sins. *Sinat chinam* is not mentioned.

But in fact, the Gemara in *Yoma* does not cite *sinat chinam* as a sin at all. It calls idolatry, illicit sexual relations and murder sins, but does not say "the sin of baseless hatred." The Gemara's attribution of the destruction of the Second Temple to *sinat chinam* is similar to R. Yochanan's attribution of it to R. Zecharia's mistakes and not to sin. *Sinat chinam* refers to the internecine warfare among the Jews, who quarreled and fought each other instead of uniting against the Romans. *Rabbeinu Chananel* in *Yoma* similarly comments that "had they ascended together [from the Babylonian exile], like a wall" they would not have been crushed, and *Maharsha* there cites the incident of Kamtza and Bar Kamtza as an example of factionalism and its consequences. Because of baseless hatred and disunity, the Temple was destroyed and we were exiled.

We can now understand the statement, "to teach you, that baseless hatred *is equal to* the three sins: idolatry, illicit sexual relations, and murder." If baseless hatred is referred to here as a sin, it would be astonishing to equate the three cardinal sins, concerning which Halacha demands that one give up one's life rather than violate and which carry the death penalty, with the relatively minor sin of hatred which is not even punishable by flogging. Rather, "is equal to (*shkulah keneged*)" involves comparison of another sort. It is found a number of times in the Talmud, such as in *Nedarim*

(25a), "The *mitzvah* of *tzitzit* is equal to all the *mitzvot* in the Torah," and (32a) "Great is circumcision, which is equal to all the *mitzvot* in the Torah," and in the Jerusalem Talmud, "*Shabbat* is equal to all the *mitzvot*."[10] Nowhere does it mean, for example, that one who wears *tzitzit* and observes nothing else is of equal merit as one who observes the rest of the Torah, or that circumcision is as important as all the other *mitzvot* put together.

Instead, "equal to" or equivalent to all the commandments means one of two things: either that certain *mitzvot* are preconditions for, or lead to observance of, all the others, as the Torah states concerning *tzitzit* "you will see it and remember all *haShem*'s *mitzvot*, and do them" (*Vayikra* 15:39). Or, that they have similar results even though they work in different ways, as the *Sifrei* in *parshat Re'eh* says, "Dwelling in the Land of Israel is equal to all the commandments." Observing *mitzvot* in the aggregate leads to awareness of G-d and so, too, does dwelling in Israel, as stated in *Ketuvot* (110b), "Everyone who lives in the Land of Israel is as if he has a Deity, as it is stated, '...to give you the land of Canaan, to be your G-d' [*Vayikra* 25:38]."

In this sense *sinat chinam* is indeed equal to idolatry, illicit sexual relations, and murder: it brought about the destruction of the Second Temple no less than the three cardinal sins brought about the destruction of the First, albeit in very different ways.

The First and Second Temples

We can now understand, as well, the comparison the Gemara makes between the two Temples, for there are three types of relationships between G-d and Israel. When Israel is wholly righteous no people or nation can rule over them, and by the same token when they are overwhelmingly wicked the opposite is true: even should the balance of forces and the international geopolitical situation seem to pose no danger, G-d will manipulate events to bring destruction upon the sinful Jewish people, as in Jeremiah (5:15), "I hereby bring a nation upon you from afar." Thus, the First Temple was destroyed in direct punishment for the sins of idolatry, illicit sexual relations, and murder; Nebuchadnezzar was "G-d's servant"[11] in carrying out His will, as before him Assyria was "the rod of My wrath."[12]

Nowhere in the Talmud, by contrast, is it claimed that G-d brought the Romans in order to destroy the Second Temple or that Titus acted as G-d's servant. During the Second Temple people were occupied with "Torah, *mitzvot*, and acts of kindness," and certainly they were not sinful enough to warrant exile as Divine punishment. However, neither were they righteous and blameless enough to merit Divine intervention to manipulate events in their favor.[13]

This marked the third type of relationship, when G-d "hides His face" and does not openly intervene. When in circumstances of *hester panim* and the absence of prophecy Israel engaged Rome in a war it could not realistically win, defeat came not as punishment for sins but because of *sinat chinam* and other natural factors. The Gemara uses identical language to ascribe the destruction to three different causes: in *Gittin* (56a), "R. Zecharia ben Avkulas' forbearance destroyed our home and burnt our sanctuary and exiled us from our land," and (57b) "The wicked kingdom (Rome) destroyed our home and burnt our sanctuary and exiled us from our land," and in *Berachot* (3a) "Because of Israel's sins I

[G-d] destroyed My home and burnt My sanctuary and exiled them among the nations." There is no contradiction, for if not for poor leadership there would have been no war, if not for a foe like Rome there would have been no defeat, and if not for Israel's modicum of sins—non-cardinal as they were—G-d would have intervened to save them.

This is the reason for the fear which resurfaces during the period of *bein hameitzarim* and *Tishah be'Av*. Had the Second Temple been destroyed as punishment for a specific sin or sins, we could, perhaps, hope and pray that we are not guilty of them today. But according to R. Yochanan and the Gemara it was destroyed despite Israel's being generally occupied with Torah, *mitzvot*, and *gemilut chassadim*, because of incompetent leadership and national disunity.[14] *Tishah be'Av* should teach us that when Israel is not wholly righteous even though not wholly wicked, we cannot be assured that G-d will save us.

"Fortunate is the man who is always afraid, and he who stiffens his heart will fall into calamity." The words are addressed to those who imagine because of what they have learned or what others have told them, that there is nothing to fear. "That refers to *divrei Torah*": Don't rely blindly on teachings or a conception or an approach or an ideology when faced with danger to *klal Yisrael*.

Notes

1. Literally, "son of Kamtza." If so, the provider of the feast was friendly with the father but antagonistic to the son, implying a severe generation gap.

2. I.e., the Roman governor of Judea.

3. Gentiles are permitted to send sacrifices to the Temple, see BT *Menachot* 73b.

4. See *Bnei Banim*, III, *ma'amar* 2, on the permissibility of violating even one of the cardinal sins to save the entire people. *Yam Shel Shlomoh*, *Yevamot* 4:9, rules that falsifying Halacha is prohibited *yeihareig ve'al ya'avor*, but he is referring to outright misrepresentation and not to merely fostering a mistaken impression as in the case of R. Zecharia, and also not to a threat to the entire nation. For an evaluation of his view see *Bnei Banim*, II, p. 43, and III, p. 146.

5. *Bamidbar Rabbah*, 20:25.

6. Alternatively: "humble." Cf. *Tosefta Shabbat* 17:4, "The school of Hillel says, 'one may remove [leftover] bones and peels from the table' (after the meal on Shabbat, in spite of *muktzah*). The school of Shammai says, 'one moves the entire table and shakes them off.' R. Zecharia ben Avkilas didn't follow either ruling, but threw them behind the bed [i.e., one peel at a time while eating, without putting any peels on the table, thus skirting the issue]. R. Yosi said, 'R. Zecharia ben Avkilus' humility (*anvatnuto*) burnt the sanctuary.'"

   R. Zecharia declined to decide between the two opinions, presumably because he did not see himself worthy of doing so, and his characteristic indecision, in the case of Bar Kamtza, caused the destruction. According to this, the proposals to sacrifice the blemished cow and to kill Bar Kamtza were two competing positions, and R. Zecharia refused to choose between them.

7. See *Teshuvot Ivra* (*Kitvei haGri"a Henkin*, vol. 2), no. 107 and *Bnei Banim*, II, p. 83 (end).

8. See note 6 above. Yet this same R. Yochanan elsewhere in *Gittin*, on pages 19a and 37a, remarked about a halachic conclusion, "Just because we imagine [such to be the law], are we going to act on it (*vechi mipnei shemidaminun na'aseh ma'aseh*)?" Evidently, although a policy of refraining from action when in doubt (*sheiv ve'al ta'aseh, adif*) is sound Halacha, it is dubious statecraft.

9. Jerusalem Talmud, *Nedarim* 9:4.

10. Ibid., *Berachot* 1:5.

11. Jeremiah 25:9; 43:10.

12. Isaiah 10:5.

13. BT *Shabbat* 119b and *Bava Metzia* 30b: "Jerusalem would not have been destroyed were it not that within it they denigrated scholars...cancelled children's Torah lessons...refrained from reciting *Shema* morning and evening..." etc. The wording "Jerusalem would not have been destroyed were it not..." (as opposed to "Jerusalem was destroyed because...") is suggestive that these sins were necessary to enable the destruction to occur, but insufficient to cause it.

14. This may explain the indeterminate length of the second Exile. In *Yoma* 9b after the comparison of the two destructions, "R. Yochanan and R. Elazar both said, 'Because the sin of the [people of the] First [Temple] was revealed, their end date was revealed (*nitgaleh avonam nitgaleh kitzam*), while because the sin of the [people of the] Second [Temple] was not revealed, their end-date was not revealed.'" That is to say, the destruction of the First Temple was manifestly a punishment for transgressing the three cardinal sins, and since G-d punished them He also notified them in advance of when the punishment would be over. But no specific sins were high-

lighted by the destruction of the second Temple, which occurred as a result of *sinat chinam* and faulty leadership as R. Yochanan himself said, and since G-d did not exile them as punishment, He also did not make it known when the exile would end.

Chapter Thirteen

THE STRENGTH TO REPENT: UNDERSTANDING EVENTS OF OUR TIME

What are we to make, theologically, of the establishment of the modern State of Israel? The crashing dissonance between the extremes of good and bad, between the restoration of Jewish national independence on the one hand and the secularization of much of Jewry on the other, has led many religious Jews to wonder how this juxtaposition can be reconciled with faith. How is it that from among all the generations, this one, so marked by abandonment of G-d's worship and violation of the *mitzvot*, was restored to its land?

One response to this problem has been to deny that it exists. There are those who dismiss the epochal nature of independence. "Jerusalem is still in *golus*!" they say (or think)—emptying the word "*golus*" (exile) of its meaning. Others stress the hopefully temporary nature of the flight from Tradition. Both positions are profoundly ahistorical and are essentially attempts at denying inconvenient reality.

A second response has been to affirm that, as in the case of the Holocaust, we are simply unable to understand G-d's reasons or purposes. But there is a limit to how much national experience we can rule off-limits to religious comprehension before we make G-d irrelevant to history altogether. Moreover, agnosticism on this issue is untenable in practice, and particularly so in Israel, where behavior often hinges on belief—one way or the other—about the role of the State in the Divine scheme of things. Without a coherent alternative we're left with a Hobson's choice of Messianism versus Satmarism,[1] most people's denial of formal adherence to the extreme positions of either notwithstanding.

Is there a third possibility, one that takes into account both the immensity of Israel's good fortune and the extent of its religious failure?

The Strength to Return

There *is* a clear and simple explanation for the restoration of Jewish sovereignty in *Eretz Yisrael* in our time. Numerous prophecies declare that Israel will not degenerate wholly into sinfulness, such as Zephaniah (3:13) "The remnant of Israel will not do evil." To prevent the destruction of the Temple and Jerusalem from leaving a religious as well as a physical wasteland in its wake, Yirmiyahu pleaded at the end of *Eichah* that G-d take the initiative: "Return us to you, *haShem*, and then we will return." The exiles lacked the strength to return, and it was necessary for G-d to take the first step.[2]

How much more did this apply to our own time, after 1,900 years of exile and 200 years of Emancipation and assimilation, after the inroads of Socialism and Communism and secularism[3] and Reform! The Jewish people was on the verge of losing its ability to do *teshuvah*. It was necessary to remove us from the countries which had bred these plagues and concentrate us in a country of our own, lest we completely lose our spiritual strength—

not to force us to repent, but to preserve our ability to do so.

We can derive from *midrashei hage'ulah* that G-d will not allow Israel to degenerate completely. Central to these *midrashim* is the dichotomy formulated by R. Yehoshua ben Levy between redemption *be'ito*, "in its appointed time" regardless of circumstances, and redemption *achishenah* which means "I will hasten," should Israel merit it (*Sanhedrin* 98a). This differentiation has been generally accepted, both because of its innate plausibility and because the prophet Eliyahu himself confirmed it in an episode related on the same page of the Talmud.

All *midrashei hage'ulah* can be classified according to R. Yehoshua ben Levy's categories. For instance, "Were Israel to observe two Sabbaths, they would be immediately redeemed" (*Shabbat* 118a) refers to a redemption *achishenah* earned by merit, which will come without delay or pre-messianic pangs. *Midrashim* such as "In the first year the rains will be selective, in the second year there will be famine," etc. (*Sanhedrin* 97a), on the other hand, describe redemption *be'ito*, in its appointed time.

What are we to make of R. Yochanan's statement, "The *Mashiach* ben David will only come in a completely worthy or completely culpable generation" (*Sanhedrin* 98a)? The former is *achishenah*, but why should the latter, a wholly culpable generation, be redeemed? Perhaps because if Israel becomes altogether wicked there is no hope for future *teshuvah*, and therefore no point in history continuing. Another explanation might be that G-d's providence is needed to prevent Israel's spiritual decay, just as R. Shimon ben Lakish said about the individual (*Sukkah* 52b); Israel as a nation would have long ago corrupted its ways, were it not for the Divine promise that "the remnant of Israel will not do evil." Prior to redemption "in its appointed time," G-d will remove His protection and Israel will degenerate of its own accord, perhaps to prove that the redemption—followed by *teshuvah*—came totally from G-d and not as a result of merit.

In any case, according to R. Yochanan the Messiah will only come when a generation is "completely worthy or completely culpable." Every generation in which *Mashiach* does *not* come, then, is neither completely worthy nor completely culpable. Just as we do not doubt that G-d performs miracles to prevent our physical extinction, for "*netzach Yisrael*" will not renege on His promise that Israel not disappear, so too we should not be surprised that He performs miracles to prevent our complete degeneration and thereby the loss of our strength to repent.

Historic Salvation

There is powerful Scriptural support for saying that G-d may initiate a historic salvation as a tactical move. We read in II Kings (14:23–27):

> In the fifteenth year of the king of Judah, Amatzyahu ben Yoash, Yeravam ben Yoash acceded to the throne in Shomron and ruled for forty-one years. He did evil in *haShem*'s view, and did not deviate from [following] all the sins of Yeravam ben Nevat who corrupted Israel. He expanded Israel's borders from Levo Chamat until the Arava Sea [the Dead Sea], in keeping with the word of *haShem*, G-d of Israel, which was spoken through His servant Yona ben Amitai of Gat-Chefer. For *haShem* saw

Israel's extremely bitter affliction and [saw] that no one
was left to lead or be led and no one was helping Israel.
HaShem had not decreed that Israel be obliterated, and
He delivered them through Yeravam ben Yoash.

We read with astonishment that Yeravam ben Yoash
followed in the footsteps of his namesake who had set up
golden calves and corrupted the ten tribes, yet he expanded the borders of the land of Israel and through him
G-d delivered Israel. His victories were of such magni-
tude that the *Sifrei* to *Devarim* (1:8) avers that the Torah
alludes to them:[4]

> "To give them"—these are the Israelites who entered the
> Land; "and to their descendants"—these are their chil-
> dren; "after them"—these are the conquests of David and
> Yeravam, as it is said, "He expanded Israel's borders
> from Levo Chamat until the Aravah Sea."

His conquests are mentioned in one breath with those of
David! How do the wicked prosper!?

The midrash *Eliyahu Rabba* (17) explains the reason
for Yeravam's achievements. In Amos (7:10–11)
Amatzia, priest of Beit-El, notified Yeravam that "Amos
is conspiring against you... This is what Amos said:
'Yeravam will die by the sword and Israel will be
exiled.'" Nevertheless, Scripture reports no action taken
by Yeravam against Amos, and the midrash elaborates:

> Yeravam rebuked Amatzia and threw him out. He told
> him, "G-d forbid, Amos never prophesied such a proph-
> ecy, and even if he did he didn't do so on his own but
> because Heaven told him to." At that moment G-d said,
> "this generation together with its leader are idolators,
> [nevertheless,] the territory I promised Abraham, Isaac,
> and Jacob that 'I will give it to your descendants' I

hereby give into the hands of this one, because he did not accept slander against Amos."

But how could non-acceptance of *lashon hara* out-weigh Yeravam's idolatry and his leading all Israel to sin?[5] By analogy, if Ben-Gurion honored the *Chazon Ish*, would that have been sufficient merit to entitle him to end the current exile?

In fact, the midrash is quite simple. The question was not whether or not to rescue Israel, for the book of Kings clearly states: "For *haShem* saw Israel's extremely bitter affliction... *HaShem* had not decreed that Israel be obliterated." G-d decided to save Israel for His own reasons, and the only question was: who should bring it about? Yeravam ben Yoash, or perhaps his father or son?[6]

Yeravam's merits were not the cause of Israel's de-liverance; rather, because of them G-d chose him and not someone else to be His instrument to save Israel. That is the meaning of the midrash's introductory question, "How was Yeravam ben Yoash different from all the kings of Israel who preceded him?" and its ending: "I hereby give [the victory] into the hands of this one [Yeravam]," i.e., and not into the hands of someone else.

This is even clearer in the midrash *Eliyahu Zuta* (7), which repeats all the above and concludes, "From this they said, good things are brought about via the worthy and bad things via the culpable. G-d applies this princi-ple to all Israel, everywhere, and to all idolaters and nations on earth." This means that G-d chooses relatively worthy people, even among idolaters, to be the vehicle of His doing good (and relatively culpable people for the opposite)—good (as well as bad) which would come about in any case.[7]

So too, in our time, G-d may have chosen sinful leaders to bring about the salvation He had already decided
upon. It is not hard to find merit in those who established
the State, even if in the final analysis they corrupted
Israel as much as did Yeravam ben Nevat and Yeravam
ben Yoash. We are not dealing with the total balance of
merit in a person, but with specific merits, or acts of
righteousness, alone.

The righteous minority who lived at the time of Yeravam ben Yoash faced a double trial. On the one hand,
they had to avoid copying his idol worship and way of
life. How easy was it to be swept away by his victories
and to conclude that his policies had proven themselves,
including, mistakenly, his idolatrous practices, for they
had expanded Israel's borders! On the other hand, the
righteous had also not to deny G-d's goodness and claim
that it was impossible for salvation to have come via a
wicked king, and that therefore the salvation they
experienced was not real, was not from G-d, and they
need not praise Him for it. The salvation was indeed
real, and with it came the obligation to praise G-d.

Many must have failed the first trial, and others the
second. Few were at the same time unswayed by the
success of the wicked and yet thankful to G-d for saving
Israel. In our day, as well, too many err in the mistaken
belief that the question of the establishment of the State
of Israel is one of our attitude to a secular state and not
of our attitude to G-d and his works. Happy are the
righteous who succeed in both trials!

Praise of the Miracle

Any comparison of our times to those of Yeravam ben Yoash is chilling, for only 26 years after his death his kingdom was destroyed by Assyria. Apparently, the existence of Shomron and its inhabitants was no longer necessary for the survival of the Jewish people. What good were Yeravam's conquests if a generation later his country was wiped out?

His victories, in fact, helped bring about the destruction, for G-d's deliverance incurs a corresponding obligation. To understand this, it should be noted that if "no one was helping Israel" was the only factor, G-d could have defeated their enemies without magnifying the victory to such an extent that Israel conquered all the way to Levo Chamat, sixty miles north (!) of Damascus. There were, however, two purposes to G-d's salvation of Israel through Yeravam: first, to remove foreign ascendancy over Israel, which corresponds to the victory in 1948, and second, to prove to Israel that G-d blesses them and seeks their good, in order to encourage them to return to Him, which corresponds to the victory in the Six Day War. G-d awakens Israel to do *teshuvah* in two ways, through punishment in order to show sinners the error of their ways and through goodness to show them G-d's love. For this reason the prophets alternate between warnings of disaster and promises of comfort and redemption.

But rescue has its costs. When foreign domination is removed, Israel can no longer claim that it is not free to worship G-d. A parallel case is described in II Kings (17:1–6):

In the twelfth year of the king of Judah, Achaz, Hoshea
ben Eilah acceded to the throne in Shomron and ruled for
nine years. He did evil in *haShem*'s sight, but not as
much as the kings of Israel who preceded him. Shalmaneser, king of Assyria, attacked him... In Hoshea's
ninth year the king of Assyria captured Shomron and exiled its inhabitants to Assyria.

The problem is obvious: if Hoshea was less wicked
than his predecessors, why was Shomron destroyed
during his reign and not during theirs? The answer is that
he permitted the ten Tribes to go on pilgrimage to the
Temple in Jerusalem for the first time since Yeravam
ben Nevat closed the borders as related in *Gittin* 88a, but
they didn't go. The midrash explains:

Until then, idol worship was connected with an individual [the king], and *haShem* is reluctant to exile the
masses for the sin of an individual. Once Hoshea ben
Eilah came and removed the border guards and proclaimed that everyone who wanted to go up to Jerusalem
could do so, but didn't *tell* them to all go up, therefore it
is recorded that "He did evil in *haShem*'s sight, but not as
much as the kings of Israel... Shalmaneser attacked him,"
because he removed the collar from his own neck and
transferred it to the neck of the people.[8]

That is to say, until the time of Hoshea the people could
blame the king for their not worshiping G-d in Jerusalem, but during his reign they had no one to blame but
themselves, and consequently were punished.

Yona ben Amitai, the prophet who foretold Yeravam's victory in II Kings (as quoted above), is the same
prophet who resisted G-d's sending him to Nineve,
capital of Assyria. Yona could hardly have thought that
if Nineve did not repent and consequently was over-

thrown Israel would then be able to escape destruction, for certainly G-d has many means at His disposal and would choose others to carry out His decrees. Rather, he refused the mission lest it result in an indictment against Israel, as the *Mechilta* (*Bo* 1) and Jerusalem Talmud (*Sanhedrin* 11:5) explain: "Yona said, 'I'll go abroad where the *Shechinah* is not revealed, because the nations repent easily,' so as not to incriminate Israel." The repentance of the residents of Nineve would highlight the obstinacy of the people of Shomron, who did not repent in spite of all the efforts of Amos and other prophets.

The Talmud (*Yevamot* 98a) derives from the verse in the book of Jonah (3:1), "The word of G-d came to Yona a second time," that G-d spoke to him only on two occasions in his life, and not more.[9] It then questions this supposition because of the verse in II Kings quoted above, "He expanded Israel's borders...in keeping with the word of *haShem*, G-d of Israel, spoken through His servant Yona ben Amitai." Wasn't that a third time G-d spoke to Yona?

R. Nachman bar Yitzchak answered that "in keeping with the word of *haShem*..." meant that "just as the fate of Nineve changed from bad to good, so Israel's fate in the time of Yeravam ben Yoash changed from bad to good." Yona's prophecy to Israel was similar to, and an extension of, his message to Nineve, and so is not counted separately. This is based on the statement in *Sanhedrin* (89b) that when G-d told Yona "Nineveh will be turned over (*nehpechet*) in forty days," Yona didn't know whether "turned over" predicted good or bad for the city: good if it meant that Nineveh would turn over a new leaf and repent, or bad if it meant that the city would be overturned and destroyed. When Nineve repented it became clear that his prophecy had foretold good for the city, and so, too, his prophecy about Yeravam foretold good for Israel.

It still seems startling to equate Yona's mission to Nineve in order that it repent, to G-d's promise conveyed through him of Yeravam's victory. If, however, G-d enabled the latter's triumphs in order to prompt Israel to do *teshuvah*, then the two prophecies are very similar. Moreover, just as Nineve's repentance served as a reproach to Israel, so too, Yeravam's successes incriminated Israel for not recognizing and not thanking G-d for His salvation. In this way the deliverance itself hastened the destruction.

The importance of thanking G-d can also be learned from King Chizkiya. In *Sanhedrin* (94a) Bar Kapara expounded:

> G-d wanted to make Chizkiya the Messiah and Sancheriv *Gog* and *Magog*. Justice protested before G-d: "...Chizkiya, for whom You performed all these miracles and [who] didn't sing a song of praise before You, will you make the Messiah?"

A song of praise (*shirah*) is one of public thanksgiving, such as *shirat hayam* which Moshe and Israel sang after the crossing of the sea and the drowning of the Egyptian army. In his private prayers Chizkiya undoubtedly gave thanks for Sancheriv's defeat, but had he aroused Israel's enthusiasm so that they publicly thanked G-d with all their hearts, their merit would have been great enough to bring the Messiah. Perhaps they didn't sing *shirah* because they were in mourning for the dead of Lachish and other Judean cities which had fallen to the Assyrians. But that was a mistake, for man must give thanks for the good, and not keep accounts with his Creator.

In *Sanhedrin* (37a) R. Hillel said, "There is no Messiah for Israel, because they already used him up in the days of Chizkiya." R. Yosef retorted "May G-d forgive him" for such an opinion, and it would indeed be amazing if R. Hillel denied the coming of the Messiah which is one of the principles of the Jewish faith.

To understand R. Hillel's statement, we must note that Chizkiya did not see himself as the Messiah nor did his contemporaries consider him as such, yet he could have become the Messiah had he and his generation sung *shirah*. R. Hillel did not deny the coming of the Messiah, but he thought that only during Chizkiya's time was there the opportunity to transform an ordinary generation into a "hastened" messianic one, and that such an opportunity would not come again prior to the coming of the Messiah in G-d's "appointed time." The Sages, who disagreed with him, held that any generation that witnesses a great salvation can bring the *Mashiach* in a hastened manner, if they sing G-d's praise with all their hearts.[10]

Chance Events

One does great evil not to thank G-d for his miracles. Such a person ascribes randomness to G-d, as *Rambam* wrote in *Hilchot Ta'anit* (1:3):

> If they don't cry out and trumpet [in distress], but say "this event is a natural occurrence and this misfortune came by chance" ...that is what is written in the Torah "I will treat you with the fury of randomness," i.e., when I

bring misfortune upon you in order that you repent, if
you claim that it is random (*keri*) I will increase the fury
of that occurrence.

Even though *Rambam* is discussing one who ascribes
disasters to chance, the same applies to one who ascribes
deliverance to chance, for both deny G-d's guiding hand.

This is what is referred to in the *tocheichah* in *Vayikra* (26:40) as "their misuse of Me and their treating Me
randomly." "Misuse (*me'ilah*)" is use of the holy for
profane purposes, and those who believe in randomness
transmute G-d's actions in the world (i.e., history),
which are manifestations of His holiness, into profane
events.

This also explains why the violation of the sabbatical
year is emphasized again and again in the *tocheichah*,
although no other specific sins are even mentioned.
"Then the land will regain its sabbaths...then the land
will lie idle and regain its sabbaths. It will lie idle...for
the time it did not lie idle during your sabbatical years
when you lived there" (26:34–5). In violating *shemittah*,
Israel denies that the country was G-d's gift to them;
they act as if they live there by chance and are not
obligated to thank G-d for it. Those who mistake G-d's
goodness for a chance event are destined to incur His
wrath, and mistake that too for chance events.[11]

One who doesn't thank G-d for His deeds commits an
additional evil. The first of the Ten Commandments is "I
am *haShem* your G-d, who took you out of Egypt"; it
means that because of the Exodus we know that He is
our G-d. The most salient proofs of the existence of G-d
are the miracles He performed. So we say at the *Pesach
seder*, "Even if we are all learned, all wise, all elders, all
conversant with the Torah, we are still required to retell

the Exodus, and the more the better." If we all know the Torah, why repeat the same things over and over? Because the Exodus is the basis for our belief in G-d, and the more we retell it the more we strengthen our faith.

Moreover, we must recount G-d's deliverances of Israel throughout history, and especially contemporary ones, since hearing or reading about salvation is not as convincing as actually seeing it. This is what is meant in Jeremiah 16:14–15 and again in 23:7–8: "No longer will it be said, '*HaShem* lives, who brought Israel up from Egypt,' but rather '*HaShem* lives, who brought Israel up from the north country and from all the countries where He had distanced them.'" "*HaShem* lives" means: *haShem* exists! The proof of His existence will be the salvation they see with their own eyes.

Let us protest against those who do not thank G-d for His salvation. The foolish imagine that there was no good done to them at all, for they haven't the heart to understand, the eyes to see nor the ears to hear what would have been the condition of Jews in the world had not the State of Israel been established in 1948, and what would have been the fate of Israel in its land were it not for the victory in 1967. Regarding them the Sages taught in the Haggada, "One must see himself as having personally left Egypt," i.e., first imagine being a slave in Egypt and only then imagine being redeemed, for one who is ignorant of the bad cannot give thanks for the good.

However, we are not protesting against the dull but against intelligent men, who know there has been a deliverance, but fear to give thanks lest they seem to approve of the secular State of Israel. Let them privately

sit in sackcloth and ashes on *Yom Haatzma'ut* and
Jerusalem Day if they want to, but they must thank G-d
at some time.[12] It seems to me that the proper time for
them to thank G-d for restoring Jewish sovereignty is at
the *seder* each year, for the story of leaving Egypt
includes the story of all the deliverances G-d wrought
throughout history. This can be learned from the Haggada: "...and that (*vehe*) is what stood our fathers and
ourselves in good stead. In every generation [enemies]
rise up to destroy us, but G-d rescues us from their
hands." The Hebrew pronoun "*he*" [fem.] refers to the
covenant (*brit* [fem.]) in *Bereishit* 15:9–18 which is
quoted directly beforehand in the Haggada, in which G-d
promised:

> Know with certainty that your descendants will be alien
> in a land not their own, and they [the inhabitants] will
> enslave and torment them [for] 400 years; I [will] also
> judge the nation that will enslave them. Afterwards they
> will leave with great wealth.

Although this seems to refer only to the bondage in
Egypt, the Sages generalized from the slavery in Egypt
to all enslavements and from the redemption from Egypt
to all redemptions. Scripture supports this by not speci-
fying Egypt or the Egyptians, but only "a land not their
own" and "the nation which will enslave them."

There are also those who refrain from praising G-d
lest their students err and be drawn to the secular State.
But they have no permission to do this, to enact *gezeirot*
to annul the obligation to praise G-d and to train students
to treat G-d with casualness and *keri* and not reflect on
His miracles.

And so, we are back to the trials that faced the generation of Yeravam ben Yoash: not to be misled by the success of the sinful, and at the same time, to acknowledge and thank G-d for his salvation.

Notes

1. Messianism views the establishment of the State of Israel as heralding the Messianic age, while Satmarism sees it as, literally, the work of Satan. On what constitutes belief in the coming of the Messiah, see *Bnei Banim*, III, *ma'amar* 3 and p. 42.

2. Zecharia (1:3) and Malachi (3:7) both said, "[first] Return to Me, and then I will return to you," but that was after *shivat Tzion*.

3. This is not the place to detail the disintegration of religious life in the shtetl, the non-Orthodox majority in Warsaw, etc., idealizations of history notwithstanding.

4. II Kings itself hints that the Torah refers to Yeravam's time. In 14:26, "no one was left to lead or be led (*ve'ephes atzur ve'ephes azuv*)" (the translation follows *Rashi* on the Torah) is virtually the same language as in *Devarim* 32:36 (*ve'ephes atzur va'azuv*)

5. A similar question is posed by the attribution in *Yoma* 9b of the destruction of the Second Temple to baseless hatred, outweighing Israel's occupation with "Torah, commandments, and acts of kindness," discussed in the previous chapter.

6. G-d normally brings about military victory through a king or general, and not through a prophet or rabbi.

7. What prompted both of these *midrashim* is II Kings 14:27, "and He delivered them through Yeravam ben

Yoash." The ending "through Yeravam ben Yoash" is
superfluous, as we already know this from 14:25. The
midrash explains that the point is that G-d effected the
rescue specifically through Yeravam, not the fact of the
rescue itself.

8.   *Yalkut Shimoni*, part II, sec. 234.

9.   The inference comes from the words "a second time"
which seem unnecessary, since we can count how many
times ourselves.

10. For the suggestion that a window of opportunity for
bringing the *mashiach* arises from time to time, see Resp.
Chatam Sofer, VI, no. 98, *s.v. Hareini*.

11. For further discussion of *keri* (mistaking G-d's acts for
random occurrences) and its causes, see my *Chibah Yeteirah: Chidushim bePeshat haTorah*, p. 65.

12. To *publicly* mourn on *Yom Haatzma'ut* and Jerusalem
Day, however, would fall under the category of "rebelling
against the nations," see *Ketuvot* 111a and *Kitvei haGri"a
Henkin*, vol. 2, p. 214, 217, in the name of R. Chaim Ozer
Grodzinski, "because the Israeli nation is also a nation."

Chapter Fourteen

IT MAY BE *GLATT*...

A confusion between two terms often used inter-
changeably today, *glatt* and *limehadrin*, offers a glimpse
into contemporary sides of an ancient problem: the
substitution of externals for internals, rote for purposeful
action, habit for *kavanah*.

The prophets grappled with this. Yeshaya (9:13) complained:

> ...because this people drew near, honored Me with their
> mouths and lips but distanced their hearts from me, and
> their worship of Me became a routine (*mitzvat anashim
> melumadah*).

Given sufficient familiarity with them, positive *mitzvot* can require little thought and can be performed while
ignoring their message. Mere technical compliance
becomes the norm—even with negative commandments.
On this *Ramban* commented:

> The Torah forbade forbidden sexual relations and forbi d-
> den foods, but permitted marital relations and consum p-
> tion of [kosher] meat and wine. The lustful person can
> therefore find room for constant relations with his wife
> or many wives, and for gorging himself on wine and
> meat... He will consequently be a knave within the letter
> of the law (*naval bireshut haTorah*).[1]

What do the terms *glatt* and *limehadrin* mean? *Glatt* in Yiddish/English or *chalak* in Hebrew, refers to an animal whose lungs are "smooth," i.e., contain no adhesions (*sirchot*) which render its kashrut questionable. In many cases the Halacha would rule that the animal is indeed kosher; nevertheless, there is a *chumra* not to rely on such rulings. In popular usage, *glatt* has taken on the meaning of rigorous standards of *kashrut* in general, even in foods such as fish or fowl where lung adhesions have no halachic significance.

Mehadrin, on the other hand, are those who perform *mitzvot* in the finest way possible. The term comes from *Shabbat* (21a):

> The *mitzvah* of Chanuka is a single light for each man and his household. Those who are meticulous (*mehadrin*), kindle a light for each member of the household. And for those who are especially meticulous (*mehadrin min hamehadrin*)—the school of Shamai states that one should kindle eight lights on the first night and subtract one every subsequent night, while the school of Hillel states that one should kindle one light on the first night and subsequently add [an additional light each night].

What is the difference between "*glatt* kosher" and "kosher *limehadrin*"? First, *glatt* refers to the food, while *mehadrin* refers to the person. Second, *glatt* is an objective quality: either the animal has lung adhesions or other problems, or it does not. *Mehadrin*, by contrast, is relative, in that what may be a sign of care in performance of the *mitzvot* in one community or generation may not be in another. Today, for instance, lighting one Chanuka candle the first night, two the second night, and so forth, following the opinion of the school of Hillel, indicates nothing particular about religious standards, since everyone lights that way.

The difference represented by *glatt* versus *mehadrin* manifests itself in unexpected ways. For example, a fancy restaurant may be *glatt* kosher, but if the food is too rich, the furnishings overly ornate, and the bill astronomical, it is hardly *limehadrin*. Those who are meticulous about peforming *mitzvot* do not waste money on such frivolities.

A *bar mitzvah* or wedding may have the finest caterer and the best rabbinical supervision, but if tens of thousands of dollars are expended on outdoing the neighbors, the affair is certainly not *limehadrin*.[2] A *mehader bemitzvot* would rather give a large or equal amount of money to *tzedakah*.

Nor is the distinction confined to matters of food. Women who dress in extravagant fashion may display the sartorial equivalent of "*glatt*" by being fully clothed and covered, but *mehadrot* know that *tzniut* (modesty) is not just a matter of not showing skin.

A publishing house behaves in a manner equivalent to "*glatt*" by declining to publish anything but pietistic works, but the effusive encomiums with which it praises its writers and sponsors are not the hallmark of *mehadrin*. The same applies to speeches at testimonials, and to the all-too-common *bar mitzvah* celebrations and pre-wedding *vorts* where rabbis, teachers, and friends vie in lauding the boy or groom to his face.

Seldom, it seems, has the gap between public endorsement of Halacha and disregard for the spirit and *midot* of Torah been as wide as today. The next time we plan or attend an affair or event, we should ask ourselves, "It may be *glatt*—but is it *limehadrin*?"

Notes

1. Commentary to *Vayikra* 19:1.

2. From time to time, Jewish communities enacted sumptu-
   ary regulations restricting the amount of guests and ex-
   penditures permitted at festive occasions; see, for example, *Ma'aseh Rav*, printed at the end of some editions of
   Resp. *Noda biYehudah*. The need was often felt to counter
   social pressures to overspend on these events.

   A recent Gerrer *Rebbe* limited not only the size of celebrations of his *chassidim*, but also the amount parents
   could spend on apartments for newlyweds. It is told that a
   wealthy follower complained to him that it was well
   within his means to spend more. The *Rebbe* retorted,
   "Then go buy yourself a different *Rebbe*."

Chapter Fifteen

WHO WILL LIVE OR DIE, *TRA LA LA*

Synagogue prayer has been a focus of esthetic interest throughout the centuries, and that has raised many problems. Writing seven hundred years ago, the *Rosh* complained of congregations that placed the cantorial skills of the *shaliach tzibur* above all other considerations:

> I was angry because *chazanim* of this country are [only] for their [the congregants'] enjoyment, to hear a beautiful voice, and they do not even care if he is a complete *rasha* just as long as he sings sweetly.[1]

A more recent problem is the use of a tuning fork on *Shabbat* by *chazanim* who wish to sing in the correct pitch. At least ten *teshuvot* over the past two hundred years addressed themselves to this question, including a brief one by my grandfather and teacher, *zeicher tzaddik livrachah*.[2] A few respondents permit the practice but most forbid it. It is rarely found today in the United States, but persists in some large congregations, particularly in Britain.

Virtually omnipresent, by contrast, is the repetition of individual syllables or entire words or phrases by the *baal tefillah*. There is no doubt that repetition of vowels is permitted, such as in the word *"ba-a-a-ruch."* Every synagogue liturgy and all Torah cantillation employ such repetition. Perhaps the reason is that most Hebrew vowels are not letters intrinsic to the text but merely signs above or below the consonants. But no such reasoning or precedent is found for repetition of consonants such as in "*atah-tah*," and even less for insertion of letters or words which are not in the text at all, such as "*oy vey.*"

The focus of rabbinical concern, however, has been on repetition of words or phrases within the liturgy. The Mishna in *Berachot* (33b) objects to the repetition "*modim, modim*" ("we will praise, we will praise"), which is taken as a sign of Dualist heresy requiring the silencing of anyone who utters it. Numerous *poskim* have objected to needless repetitions of any sort, either because they indicate that the *chazan* is infatuated with his musical prowess or because of a possible *hefsek*, or breach, which can invalidate the prayer.[3]

What about the tunes themselves—can they be from non-Jewish sources? Actual church music is inadmissible, as are melodies from erotic songs,[4] but secular or even non-Jewish origins *per se* do not disqualify tunes from use in the synagogue, as long as the worshipers do not recall the original words while mouthing the Hebrew liturgy. Those who, after the Six Day War, sang *Lechah Dodi* to the tune of *Yerushalayim shel Zahav*, caused their congregations to focus on "the road to Jericho" rather than the Sabbath Queen!

Today, the Orthodox community is blessed with composers who produce original music for all parts of the service. Not only do traditional songs such as *Lechah Dodi* and *Keil Adon* have a plethora of new tunes, but so do prayers that have rarely if ever been sung in the past, and this itself has become a problem. Eight hundred years ago, *Sefer Chassidim* instructed:

> Seek out one of the melodies, and when you pray, speak in a melody that is pleasant and sweet in your eyes. Say your prayers in that melody, and you will pray with devotion and your heart will be drawn after what your lips utter. For words of beseeching and request, [find] a melody that makes the heart cry, and for words of praise, [find] a melody that gladdens the heart, so that your mouth will be filled with love and happiness for Him who sees your heart. [5]

Particularly on the High Holidays, which are times of "beseeching and request," we hear tunes that do not do justice to, and sometimes conflict with, the majesty and pathos of the prayer texts. For example, the exalted prayer *Unetaneh Tokef*, the sublime and terrifying high point of the *Musaf* service:

> A great trumpet will be sounded and a still small voice will be heard. The angels will be alarmed, fear and trembling will seize them, and they will say, "This is the day of judgment..."
>
> [Judgment] will be written on Rosh Hashana and sealed on the fast of Yom Kippur: how many will pass away and how many will be created, who will live and who will die, who [will die] in his proper time and who not in his proper time, who by water and who by fire, who by sword and who by wild beast, who by starvation and who by thirst... Who will be tranquil and who agitated, who will have peace and who be afflicted, who will be impoverished and who made rich, who brought low and who raised high.

In too many synagogues today, this is sung to sweet tunes, nostalgic tunes, tunes that are the equivalent of singing, "Who will live and who will die, *tra la la*." Men and women emerge from such a service and sigh "How beautiful!"—as if that were the measure of the day.

Or consider *Tefilat Geshem*, the prayer for rain said during *Musaf* on *Shemini Atzeret*. One tune in use is a lilting, soft melody which sticks in the throat when sung to the last stanza:

> Remember the twelve tribes, whom You brought through the split waters; You sweetened the bitterness of water for them. The blood of their descendants has been spilled like water for Your sake.

Our generation is capable of singing of Jewish blood spilled like water and noticing only the music.

The solution is not to forgo melodies altogether. Congregations that have ceased singing even *Lechah Dodi* to any recognizable melody in the mistaken belief that chanting rather than singing is somehow "more religious," have misread the legacy of thousands of years of prayer originating in the *Beit haMikdash* itself. But the message must fit the chime. We must guard against musical notes taking precedence over words, tunes over text, against estheticism overshadowing communication with G-d—in sum, against letting beauty mask vacuity in the vocal equivalent of a golden calf.

Notes

1. *Teshuvot haRosh*, 4:22.

2. *Teshuvot Ivra* (*Kitvei haGri"a Henkin*, vol. 2), no. 14.

3. The responsa tend to differ only in the degree of severity with which the phenomenon is viewed, cf. Resp. *Maharam Shick, Orach Chayim*, no. 31 and Resp. *Igrot Moshe, Orach Chayim*, II, no. 22. My grandfather considered wordless *nigunim* to be a *hefsek* in prayer, unless done out of spontaneous religious fervor; see *Eidut leYisrael, Ikarei Dinim*, par. 64, reprinted in *Kitvei haGri"a Henkin*, vol. 1, p. 124a (161) and see Resp. *Bnei Banim*, II, p. 211, par. 36.

4. *Rama* in *Orach Chayim* 53:25 is not directly discussing the use in prayer of tunes from erotic songs, but rather a cantor who sings erotic songs on the side and is therefore unfit to officiate at prayer; see Resp. *Rif* (Bulgaria edition), no. 39; *Orchot Chayim, Orach Chayim, Hilchot Tefillah*, par. 78. The tunes themselves would certainly be objectionable, however (*hakrivu na lifechatecha*).

5. No. 158; Parma edition, no. 11.

BIOGRAPHY

Chapter Sixteen

RABBI YOSEF ELIYAHU HENKIN זצ"ל

I. In Europe

At the end of the 19th century, 700,000 Jews lived in White Russia (Byelorussia) in northwest Russia. They constituted 12% of the total population and were a majority in the cities. The major cities were Minsk (47,000 Jews), Vitebsk (35,000), and Mogilev and Pinsk (21,000 each).

White Russia was the center of "Lithuanian" Jewry and most of the Lithuanian yeshivot were located there, in small towns such as Volozhin (2,510 Jews) and Mir (3,500); there were 10,000 Jews in Slutzk, 5,000 in Shklov and about half that in Shtoptsi. A village in Mogilev province, Lubavitch, was also the cradle of *Chabad* Chassidism.

Of the 200,000 Jews in Mogilev province, 39% earned a living from trade, 35% from crafts, and about 5% from agriculture in some 70 villages. In all, 39% of the Jews lived in the province's larger towns, 38% in the smaller towns, and 23% in the villages. About 5,000 Jews each lived in Rogachev and Shklov and half that in Climovicz and Kritchof.[1]

Eliyahu Yosef Henkin was born in Climovicz in White Russia near the border with Russia, on *motza'ei Shabbat*, the first day of *Rosh Chodesh Adar Aleph* 5641 (1881), the third child and first boy in a family which would number four brothers and four sisters.[2] His father, R. Eliezer Klonymus, was *rosh yeshiva* in Climovicz and his father's father, Avraham, was a teacher. Avraham's father, Yitzchak, lived to be almost a hundred and was a *ben Torah*, as were his descendants. Eliyahu Yosef did not know his more remote ancestors, but heard that they were of distinguished lineage.

Eliyahu Yosef was known as a prodigy in *Tanach* at the age of three. He first studied *Tanach* for a year with his great-grandfather and the following year with his grandfather, and afterwards studied Talmud and other subjects for three years with his father. He then spent a year in the yeshiva of the rabbi of Climovicz, Rabbi Zvi Hirsh Lifshitz, and two years in the yeshiva of his future father-in-law, Rabbi Yehuda Leib Kreindel, the rabbi of Kritchof, whose only surviving responsum is printed in *Lev Ivra*.[3] May the memory of all be for a blessing.

After his *bar mitzvah* he studied by himself in Climovicz for two years, learning *seder Moed* numerous times, attending the local rabbi's lectures and studying with the rabbi's son and another youth. At fifteen he traveled to the Mir yeshiva but found it overcrowded, and studied for a year in Karelitz. Afterwards he went to Slutzk.

The yeshiva in Slutzk had been founded that same year (1897) by Rabbi Isser Zalman Meltzer—who brought with him fourteen of the Slobodka yeshiva's best students (all considerably older than Eliyahu Yosef)—with the encouragement of the rabbi of Slutzk, the *gaon Ridba"z*. As an entrance exam, the *rosh yeshiva* opened tractate *Eiruvin* and asked what was written on various pages. Eliyahu Yosef had already learned *Eiruvin* as many as fourteen times, and he enumerated the *tanaim* and *amoraim* and their discussions on each page until the *rosh yeshiva* exclaimed that the youth knew the tractate better than he did.

He studied in Slutzk for six years. Rabbi Meltzer, ten years his senior, became an admirer and friend. When the *rosh yeshiva* traveled out of town he entrusted the yeshiva's daily affairs to him. At the age of twenty, he was ordained by the *Ridba"z*, by Rabbi Baruch Ber Leibovitz, rabbi of Halusk and subsequently head of the Slobodka yeshiva, and by Rabbi Yechiel Michel Epstein, rabbi of Novharadok and author of the *Aruch haShulchan*, may their memories be a blessing. Rabbi Baruch Ber's examination lasted several days, and when writing the *semichah* certificate he remarked that he was writing it with happiness.

When Rabbi Henkin left the yeshiva, R. Meltzer presented him with a copy of the book *Levush Mordechai* on *Bava Kama*, with the following inscription in Hebrew:[4]

> This book is a present to my dear and beloved, *harav haGaon*, *sinai* [repository of knowledge] and *oker harim* [mover of mountains], treasury of Torah and fear of Heaven, of outstanding talent and destined for prominence and glory in Israel: our honorable mentor Rabbi Elia Henkin, who has learned for six years in this great academy. Our yeshiva can take pride that it has produced such a *gadol*. May it be His will that you continue with this impetus and rise to the level of the *gaonim* of the generation on whom Israel prides itself. Your admirer and friend, Isser Zalman Meltzer.

Years afterwards, the *gaon* R. Meltzer addressed correspondence to "my friend and cherished *haGrai"h*," and Rabbi Henkin always referred to him as "my teacher and rabbi."

At age 21, he became engaged to Rabbi Kreindel's daughter, Rivka. The wedding took place in Kritchof fifteen months later, on Thursday, 9 *Sivan* 5663 (1903).

During their first ten years of marriage, he and his wife lived in ten different places. A year after the wedding he returned to Slutzk. Shortly afterwards he traveled to the Caucasus, to Georgia, through arrangements made by his father-in-law.[5]

Georgia was then a province of Russia, on the Black Sea near the Turkish border, 900 miles from White Russia. Eighteen thousand Jews lived there and the largest community, Kutais, numbered 5,000. Almost all the Jews in Georgia were Sephardim, and they had some unusual customs: women did no work and prepared no food from the onset of menstruation until the beginning of their clean days. They would decorate a sick person and themselves and dance and burn incense to ward off demons. Men decorated the dead, placed provisions and money in the grave and recited the *shehecheyanu* blessing during burial. On Purim, they wished each other a good year. Resp. *Divrei Malkiel*, vol. 5, nos. 100–5 and 249–51, were written to the young Rabbi Henkin in answer to his questions on these and other matters. Yet he found in Georgia many positive prayer and synagogue practices, which he subsequently cited in *Eidut leYisrael*.[6]

He first lived for four years in the town of Oni, and spread Torah and *yirat shamayim* as a *moreh hora'ah* and *rosh metivta*. He clarified how to write the town's

name in writs of divorce and dealt with matters of *treifot*,
levirate marriage as was customary in Georgia, *eiruvin*
and many other halachic questions. Years later he used
to say that he became expert in *hora'ah* during his years
in the Caucasus.

Georgian Jews esteemed him, and over fifty years
after he left, a sign still hung in the Oni slaughterhouse:
"Slaughterers must examine each other's knives, by
directive of Rabbi Eliyahu Yosef Henkin."[7] When the
first emigrants from Soviet Georgia came to New York
in the 1960s they visited his apartment and knelt and
kissed his hand. Although born long after he had left
Georgia, they had been instructed by their fathers to
honor him wherever he was.

After leaving Oni, he served briefly as a *rosh metivta*
in the yeshiva founded in the town of Tzachinval (later
called Stalinir[8]) by Rabbi Avraham Halevi Chawalis *z"l*,
one of several Ashkenazic rabbis in Georgia. Afterwards
he spent three years in Kulash as a *rosh metivta* and
moreh hora'ah. While there he described the state of the
local rabbinate as follows:

> Among our Sephardic brethren the *chacham* functions as
> a cantor, synagogue administrator, ritual slaughterer, and
> teacher. *Hora'ah* comes automatically, and our simple
> and wholesome brethren believe a *chacham* knows every
> secret... All the Ashkenazic rabbis, except for the rabbi
> of Tzachinval, have been appointed, not as rabbis and
> *morei hora'ah*, but as Talmud teachers. Not authorized
> by the government, they must depend on the official
> *chachamim* to permit them to arrange marriages and di-
> vorces. Not all *chachamim* recognize them [the Ash-
> kenazic rabbis], however, and many of these
> [*chachamim*] presume to arrange marriages and divorces
> and rule and judge on halachic matters they know not h-

ing about. The *gedolei hador*, *shlit"a*, should remove this stumbling block... However, the rabbi of Kutais, the *chacham* Reuven, will be remembered positively for vigorously attempting to prevent such *chachamim* from arranging marriages and divorces.[9]

During this period he ruled that the local practice of giving an engagement ring necessitated a divorce if the engagement was broken. The *gaonim* Rabbi Malkiel Tzvi Halevi of Lomza in Poland, author of Resp. *Divrei Malkiel*, and Rabbi Chaim of Brisk and others (may their memories be a blessing) agreed with him, as he reported in *Peirushei Ivra*.[10]

He was eventually forced to leave Kulash for lack of a residence permit. With the permission of the local authorities he was appointed rabbi of Akhaltzikhe, but the provincial governor opposed the appointment. After a short period as a *rosh metivta* in Kutais, he and his family returned to White Russia in late 1913.

He visited Rabbi Meltzer who in the meantime had become rabbi of Slutzk, and his teacher traveled with him to help find him a rabbinical position.[11] In *Tishrei* 5674 (1914) Rabbi Henkin delivered a homily while seeking the rabbinate in the town of Maholna, portions of which became the third article in the second section of *Peirushei Ivra* and the introduction to which was recently published.[12] Rabbi Meltzer arranged his appointment as a *rosh yeshiva* in Shtoptsi, the city of Rabbi Yoel Sorotzkin, *z"l*. Soon afterwards he was appointed *rosh yeshiva* in the yeshiva in Shklov which was founded by the *gaon* Rabbi Meir Schwartz, *z"l*.

In late 1914 he was chosen rabbi of Smolien, a town in the Vitebsk province in White Russia.[13] He served there for nine years. In his notebook he recorded local births, deaths, weddings, etc., and summarized his halachic rulings in over forty difficult cases brought before him, most of them regarding monetary matters.[14] He was already known as an expert in *hora'ah*, and rabbis from nearby communities turned to him to conduct judicial proceedings.

At the end of World War I and during the Russian revolution, Russian and Polish armies fought each other in White Russia. Thefts and robberies were rampant, and on the 10th of *Tevet* 5678 (1918) Rabbi Henkin and his community proclaimed a ban (*cherem*) both on thieves and on their Jewish accomplices who failed to return stolen goods. A more far-reaching ban was issued in *Cheshvan* 5679, on "whosoever delivers Jewish persons or property over to robbers, whether actively or by brazen incitement." In addition, the community suffered from gentile drunkenness, and therefore outlawed the sale by Jews to gentiles of both whiskey and the malt and yeast used in making whiskey.

In Smolien his wife Rivka, weakened by dysentery, died after her seventh birth. He wrote the following in his notebook:

> My friend and partner, the light of my eyes and my crown; who can find such a woman of valor, who loved me with all her being and devoted herself to providing all the necessities of the home while wandering near and far amid great hardship and physical frailty? Her soul returned to G-d who had given it, on *Shabbat*, 7 *Elul* 5680. May her soul be bound in eternal life, and may her merit protect all her descendants.
>
> She was eight months pregnant when the epidemic broke out in town. There was no one to distribute food to the sick so she did so herself, and she contracted the dis-

ease... and died shortly after giving birth. The baby, named Rivka after her mother, died within a month.

She left three daughters and three sons, among them my father.

In 1921, half of White Russia was annexed by Soviet Russia. In the winter of 1923, the authorities came to press Rabbi Henkin into physical labor, and desisted only when the town's Jews demanded that they also take the local priest.

With his second wife, Chana, daughter of Yaakov Lev Kazachkov *z"l*, he left Russia for America with the help of his brother-in-law Chaim Tzvi who lived in the United States. Rabbi Henkin distributed most of his library to residents of Smolien, and during Chanuka he and his family boarded a train to Latvia, thence to Cherbourg in France from where they sailed for the United States. They were held by immigration authorities on the "Isle of Tears" (Ellis Island) for five weeks, and released through a bond posted by Levi, son-in-law of Mrs. Lookstein of Smolien. May the memory of all of these people be a blessing, and may G-d reward all those who do good.

II. In America

In New York, Rabbi Henkin became rabbi of Congregation *Anshei Shtutzin uGrayeva* on the Lower East Side,[15] and during this time published *Peirushei Ivra* (c. 1925), parts of which he had written in Europe. The book analyzes and explains the categories of betrothal and marriage, witness and presumption (*chazakah*), and concludes with a proposal concerning *agunot*; the second half is *derashot*. It is basic to an understanding of the status of betrothals and civil marriages, and should be read together with the study of *seder Nashim*.

Ivra is an acronym of Eliyahu Yosef ben R. Eliezer (Klonymus), his name from birth.[16] In Europe in 1917, he had already entitled a section of his notebook "*Likutei Ivra*." His contemporaries such as R. Meltzer continued to write to him under the name of Eliyahu Yosef, but in America the order of his names became reversed, to Yosef Eliyahu.

Serving as a synagogue rabbi was not enough to occupy him, as he wrote to his father-in-law, nor to support his family. In *Tammuz* 5685 (1925) he was appointed director of Ezras Torah, succeeding R. Baruch Epstein, the author of the *Torah Temimah*.[17] Ezras Torah had been founded ten years earlier at the beginning of the first World War by the Agudas Harabbonim with the assistance of the Mizrachi movement, to support rabbis, scholars, and their families in Europe and elsewhere, who were refugees or otherwise in need. Its first president was the *gaon* R. Yisrael Rosenberg *z"l*, who served until his death in 1956.

Rabbi Henkin directed Ezras Torah for 48 years until his death. Some $6,000,000 was raised and distributed under his direction, including $300,000 during the years 5685–95, the period of the worldwide great depression; $1,300,000 during 5696–5706 which spanned the Holocaust; and $1,500,000 during 5708–15 which saw the creation of the State of Israel. The sums were contributed by rabbis and laymen, men and women, often through small appeals in synagogues, at breakfasts and through neighborhood women's groups and the like. Ezras Torah did not have large contributors or paid fund-raisers. It was similar in this respect to the Western

Wall of the Temple which, according to folk-legend, was built by the common people and as a result was never destroyed.

It became a popular aphorism that "All charities are holy, but Ezras Torah is the holy of holies." During the difficult years after the first World War the *gaonim* of Europe such as the *Chafetz Chayim*, R. Chaim Ozer Grodzinski of Vilna and R. Avraham Duber Cahana-Shapira of Kovno, of blessed memory, called on Ezras Torah to assist them in their localities. Its renown spread throughout the world, and with it spread word of the devotion and righteousness of its director, the *gaon* R. Yosef Eliyahu Henkin.

He worked full-time in its office for forty-two years. On *Shabbat* he walked to synagogues to conduct appeals, and in the summer and occasionally in the winter, too, he traveled to cities such as Baltimore and Rochester and to hotels in the mountains. He took kosher food with him and spent *Shabbat* in remote communities to collect for Ezras Torah.

For many years he refused to accept a raise in salary, particularly after he reached age 65 and began to receive social security. Once the board of trustees of Ezras Torah insisted on giving him a raise, and at the end of the year found an unexpected surplus in the bank, for R. Henkin hadn't cashed some of his salary checks in order to avoid receiving it.[18] "Those we support need the money more than I do," he said.

When he was seventy-five years old, a convocation of rabbis presented him with a ticket to travel to Israel, where he had never been. He refused to go unless they also gave him many thousands of dollars to distribute to needy scholars there, above and beyond their normal contributions—and ended up not going.

He often ended his written and oral *teshuvot* with a request to help Ezras Torah. He donated the proceeds of *dinei Torah* and divorce-proceedings to Ezras Torah. Books of his in Halacha were appended to anniversary volumes of the institution. The synagogue calendar of Ezras Torah, edited according to his rulings and directions, is the most widely used in the United States. He expended all his efforts on Ezras Torah, until he considered it a part of his being and his heart was bound up with its functioning and expansion.[19]

He was meticulous in maintaining the ledgers of the institution, and accountants verified that every penny was entered in the books. Receipts were mailed punctually. Ezras Torah kept secret the names of those it supported, and Rabbi Henkin was careful to greet everyone with respect, whether recipient or donor, and to turn no one away empty-handed without at least a token sum. The larger sums, however, were distributed according to the need and worthiness of the recipient, as Ezras Torah's primary function was to assist scholars and their families.

Rabbi Henkin was famous as a *gadol hador* and one of a handful of supreme arbiters of practical Halacha in America. His rulings on matters of *Shabbat* and electricity were widely accepted by the religious community. He was the final authority in *gittin*, and rabbis in many countries turned to him in difficult cases. He impressed upon the consciousness of rabbinic authorities the halachic consequences of civil marriages, requiring a *get* in addition to a civil divorce.

When the *gaon* Rabbi Aharon Kotler was asked if wordless singing was an interruption in prayer, at first he answered in the negative; when told that *Rav* Henkin forbade it, he replied, "If so, then I also forbid it." Rabbi A. Z. Halperin, founder of the Center for Family Purity, after immigrating to Israel in 1936 told his son-in-law, "There is one rabbi in America one can address questions to, and he is *haGri"a* Henkin." The *Admo'r*, Rabbi Yosef Yitzchak of Lubavitch, declined to answer when queried on a certain matter of Halacha, and said, "Ask a rabbi." Asked who was such a rabbi, he answered "A rabbi like *Rav* Henkin." One *gadol* mentioned that in divorce proceedings in Europe he used to act in a certain manner, but here "*Rav* Henkin doesn't permit it."

Rabbi Henkin was called, simply, "*Rav* Henkin," without further honorific title. He was the rabbi of other rabbis, and from all over North America rabbis wrote or telephoned him when problems arose in their communities. A number of *yeshivot* gave his telephone number to their graduates together with their *semichah* certificates, Rabbis from the New York area came to him to arrange divorces for their congregants, and hundreds were arranged in the office of Ezras Torah and in his home. Dozens of rabbis gathered with him every *erev Pesach* to sell *chametz*, each bringing numerous powers-of-attorney.

I fulfilled the *mitzvah* of *chalitzah* in his home. In the days preceding the ceremony I noticed that two variations of the *chalitzah*-shoe seem to be described in the *poskim*, although this is nowhere stated explicitly; subsequently, I found he had both.

In 5796 (1936) in the 20th anniversary volume of Ezras Torah, he published an abridgment of laws for the whole year together with articles and comments for practical application. He footnoted, "All this has been written by the director of Ezras Torah, and if anyone should find a law in it which is not in accordance with Halacha, let me know so that I can justify it or admit [the mistake]." In 5706 (1946) he expanded the material by 50 percent and printed it in the 30th anniversary volume called *Eidut leYisrael*, from where it was cited extensively in books such as *Shaarim Hametzuyanim be-Halacha* and *Yesodei Yeshurun*. In 5716 (1956), again in an anniversary volume of Ezras Torah, he published 32 articles under the name *Lev Ivra* (לב=32) plus another 16 articles in Yiddish.

In addition to working full-time in Ezras Torah, Rabbi Henkin published dozens of halachic articles in rabbinical journals, and many others in matters of *hashkafah* and *chesed*. He wrote frequently in Yiddish newspapers on Jewish affairs. He followed the news, was well-versed in Jewish history and was knowledgeable in politics and other worldly affairs. In the initial anniversary volume of Ezras Torah in 1926 he published a chronology from the Creation to the present day, together with a list of *poskim* in each generation which he copied from Resp. *Chavalim Bene'imim* together with his own additions, comments and references. He wrote that he would have compiled his own list altogether, had he not been concerned about slighting those whose names he would have had to leave out for lack of space.

Ordinary men and women telephoned him or came to his apartment, asked questions and requested blessings. His was an open house, and he had no doorkeeper. Rabbi Henkin greeted everyone pleasantly and sent them away with words of blessing, and answered simple questions in the same respectful way that he answered difficult ones. He acted the same on the telephone; however, for many years he would ask the caller if there was a recognized rabbi in his vicinity. If so, he would suggest that the caller first consult locally, so as not to undermine the local rabbinate.

In *Eidut leYisrael* he commented on many widespread customs and practices.[20] He had acute powers of discernment. Often, in his *teshuvot*, he correctly surmised circumstances the questioner did not make clear. It was difficult to fool him and impossible to cajole him. Once, when he saw an editorial in a rabbinical journal calling for the establishment of an organization of rabbis to oversee *kashrut*, he dryly remarked that he had made the same proposal many years previously: *then* rabbis weren't interested, but *now* that a lay organization had succeeded in the task, rabbis wanted it for themselves. After someone telephoned him to ask whether a stratagem to circumvent travel tax from a certain country was permissible or not, he turned and said, "This person wants to sin, and wants me to be his partner?"

He had a fine sense of humor and liked to laugh, but didn't open his mouth wide, in keeping with R. Yochanan's dictum that it is forbidden to fill one's mouth with laughter in this world.[21] He enjoyed singing, and we sang *zemirot* on *Shabbat* with him even after he was ninety, and similarly after the family reading of the *megillah* each year. After the Passover *seder* a year before his passing, my wife told him how much she enjoyed his tune for *chasal sidur Pesach*. He replied that he had learned it from the *Ridba"z* in Slutzk, and sang it over again from beginning to end.

He gave himself little credit, and when asked why
tzaddikim are afraid of death—is not paradise reserved
for them?—replied, "Who says I'm a *tzaddik*?" Once he
commented on the fact that he had never visited *Eretz*
Israel, and said that perhaps it was for the best, as they
would expect him to give a *shiur* there and perhaps
would be disappointed in him. He did not stand on
honor; once, in his seventies, when a cantor was delayed
at a wedding he acted as cantor and sang the introductory verses himself.

When Rabbi Henkin reached the age of eighty, he
wrote in his will that he should have a gravestone the
same size as that of his first son Chaim Shimi, who died
as a youth in 5697 (1937), and in the same cemetery, and
not to indulge in titles but to inscribe simply "Rabbi
Yosef Eliyahu ben R. Eliezer Klonymus Henkin, author
of *Peirushei Ivra* and *Lev Ivra*, formerly rabbi of various
communities in Russia and in this country of Cong.
Anshei Shtutzin uGrayeva, and director of the holy
institution Ezras Torah," and this was done. He willed to
be buried in the United States so that American Jewry
not be bereft of the graves of its rabbis.

In his final years when his sight gave out, rabbis and
students came and learned with him. He corrected their
readings in Gemara, *Rashi*, and *Tosafot*, and cited
poskim and chapters in *she'elot uteshuvot* years after he
had last seen them. He was fluent in Hebrew, and I
learned with him completely in Hebrew.

He continued to rule on halachic questions and to
dictate articles and letters. He went to work daily in
Ezras Torah, and when finally unable to leave his home,
his office came to him. *Gittin* and other matters continued to be arranged there. His neighbors *davened* in his

study every morning and on *Shabbat* and holidays, may their merit protect those who remain. Rabbi Shizgal *z"l* davened there until his passing. Mr. Shmuel Morowitz *z"l* was the *gabai* of the minyan, and Mr. Miller *z"l* who attended him in his home should also be remembered.

He was decisive until the end,[22] and in his last year he withstood the pressures which both sides to a famous controversy applied on him.[23] He stressed practical matters to the *gedolim* and *roshei yeshivot* who visited him, such as the prohibition of eating before *shofar*-blowing[24] and the obligation of the *shaliach tzibur* to bless "*gaal Yisrael*" aloud.[25]

After *Musaf* on *Shabbat Nachmu*, 13 *Av* 5733 (August 11, 1973), Rabbi Henkin died a peaceful death in his chair in his study, which served as a synagogue in his final years. He was 93 years old and the oldest of the *gaonim* of his generation. Tens of thousands attended his funeral. One *rosh yeshiva*[26] cried, "I had been certain that he would live to receive the Messiah for us. Now who will receive him?" He was eulogized throughout America and in Bnei Brak and Jerusalem, where a synagogue was built in his memory.

In my studies with him during his last years, when I reached chapter four of *Menachot* concerning the sky-blue (*techeilet*) strands of *tzitzit* (ritual fringes) which are not a precondition for the white strands, he noted that *tzitzit* is mentioned in two places: in *Bamidbar* (15:38) "They shall put a sky-blue strand on the corner fringe," and in *Devarim* (22:12) "You shall make fringes on all four corners." In the first verse sky-blue is mentioned but not four corners, while in the second, four corners are mentioned but not sky-blue, which implies that the basic obligation of *techeilet* is on a single corner.[27] I reflected that this implication applied also to him, and silently vowed to say so after the fullness of his years. G-d helped me keep my vow, and I arrived from Israel at the funeral in New York during the eulogies.

For just as there are *gedilim* (fringes) so are there *gedolim* (great men); a generation may have many *gedolim*, each with his own attributes but, nonetheless, essentially similar to each other. Once in a generation or a few generations, however, there appears one who by virtue of his combination of attributes and unique characteristics resembles a sky-blue strand and has no equivalent. *Rabbeinu*, my grandfather and teacher, was a sky-blue strand.

III. An Appreciation

Fearlessness of opinion, unaffected simplicity, blameless piety—for these and other attributes Rabbi Yosef Eliyahu Henkin was revered by communities spanning more than one generation and continent.[28] His was a life of selfless service based on Torah and devotion to his people.

He was blessed with a genius' intelligence and an extraordinary memory, and with unusual originality in thought and action, an embodiment of the verse in Proverbs (5:16), "Your springs of water will burst outwards (*yafutzu ma'ayanotecha chutzah*), [resulting in] streams of water in the streets."[29] A preeminent halachic authority, he was so personally devoted to the welfare of Jews and of Israel that it was hard to determine which was greater, his scholarship or his righteousness.

The Torah says: "You shall come to the Levitical priests and to the judge who will be (*asher yihyeh*) in those days" (*Devarim* 17:9). The Talmud asks:[30] can one conceive of going to a judge who is *not* in his days? One might also ask why the Torah says *asher yihyeh*, "who will be in those days," rather than simply *asher*, "who is"?

But in fact there can be a judge who lives in a generation but is not of it, in that he doesn't understand its circumstances and problems. The Torah stipulates "the judge who will be in those days," because one must seek a judge who is familiar with contemporary conditions. Moreover, the judge himself is commanded to be acquainted with society, hence the extra word "*yihyeh*," "who *shall* be in those days." Rabbi Henkin was a judge for his day and ours, conversant with Jews, society, and contemporary needs.

He wrote in his will concerning Ezras Torah:

> There is no room in it [Ezras Torah] for mere intellectual exercises (*pilpulim*). I applied to this the statement of our Sages that Rabbi Eleazar ben Arach was drawn to Prugita wine and Diomsit water, and when he returned he misread "*hachodesh hazeh lachem*" ("this month is for you" [*Shemot* 12:2]) as "*hecheireish hayah libam*" ("their heart was deaf").[31] For his strengths had been his originality and his great heart, but in his excesses he squandered his originality on empty novellae for his own amusement, and his good heart was weakened. Finally the Sages prayed for him, and both qualities were returned to him together.

So, too, in Torah and in *chessed*, *Rabbeinu* measured matters by their practicality and benefit. He championed the study of Halacha neglected in his day, and wrote *haskamot* only for books dealing with Jewish law. He criticized the ordination of rabbis proficient only in

Yoreh De'ah and the tractates customarily studied in the *yeshivot*, and required knowledge of *Orach Chayim*, the Order of *Mo'ed*, *Mishnayot* and *Tanach*.

He himself dwelt in the "four cubits of Halacha," which refer, not to the innermost rooms of a private domain, but rather to the alleyways outside and to the peripheries of a public domain.[32] He occupied himself with the needs of the community in Russian Georgia, in Smolien, and finally through Ezras Torah, which sustained thousands of destitute scholars and their families all over the world before and after World War II.

He published dozens of articles on current halachic questions and contemporary issues in journals and newspapers, and issued frequent statements on matters of general concern. After its establishment he publicly protested against the extreme religious opponents of the fledgling State of Israel; he himself neither loved nor hated the State, but was concerned for the safety of its inhabitants.[33] He honored *talmidei chachamim* everywhere, cast no aspersions on recognized rabbis and belonged to no party or political faction. He was considered a *gaon* in an age of *gaonim* and a *tzaddik* among *tzaddikim*.

Rabbi Henkin explained the verse, "Noah was a righteous person, he was wholesome in his generations" (*Bereishit* 6:9) as follows: Noah lived through both the flood and the tower of Bavel. In the generation of the flood, which was marked by evil between men, Noah was nonetheless righteous to others.[34] In the generation of the tower of Bavel which was wicked to Heaven, on the other hand, Noah remained wholesome to G-d. Thus, he was exemplary "*bedorotav*" (in the plural), "in [both] his generations."[35]

Through this explanation we can reconcile the Sages' seemingly contradictory statements, on the one hand that Noah was exemplary in comparison to his own generation but not in comparison to others, and on the other hand that he was even *more* exemplary in comparison to other generations.[36] They refer to different aspects of Noah's righteousness. In Avraham's time Noah's relationship to G-d would not have been considered outstanding, because Avraham was a greater believer than he. But regarding other people, if Noah was blameless even in relating to the wicked, he would have been so much the more blameless in a less depraved generation.

A fitting explanation by *Rav* Yosef Eliyahu Henkin, my grandfather, of blessed memory, who was both righteous to people and wholesome to Heaven!

Notes

1.   Statistics based on the 1897 Russian census, collated from the *Jewish Encyclopedia* (1901-1906) and *Encyclopaedia Judaica* (1972), *s.v.* Belorussia, Mogilev, Russia *et al.*

2.   These and other details of R. Henkin's family and life in Europe have been copied from his private notebook from Smolien, now in this writer's possession, or are personal recollections conveyed orally. See *Bnei Banim*, II, pp. 208–11, *"Imrei haGaon R. Yosef Eliyahu Henkin zatza"l,"* nos. 1–5, 8–9, 46 and note on p. 208. The recollections there include remarkable observations on *gedolim* of his time.

3.   Pp. 79–87. Rabbi Kreindel, but not his son-in-law, was affiliated with *Chabad*-Lubavitch.

4. Now in this writer's possession.

5. My aunt, Mrs. Dora Weber *a"h*, recalled that on arrival in Georgia they were met at the train station by local notables and a brass band.

6. Pp. 134, 155, 161, and esp. 159.

7. Reported by Georgian immigrants in Jerusalem.

8. In honor of its native son. According to one account, R. Henkin related having ridden in a wagon with the young Stalin, who spoke approvingly of Jews. However, after a few drinks at an inn Stalin expressed himself rather differently. See Ben Zion Shurun, *Keshet Giborim*, p. 78.

9. Rabbi Shmuel N. Gottlieb, *Ohalei Shem*, Pinsk, 5672 (1912), *s.v.* Henkin, Rabbi Elia Yosef. The book is a directory of rabbis active at the time. R. Henkin, then in Smolien, was perhaps the last to pass away from among those listed.

10. P. 109. Also see Resp. *Atzei haLevanon*, no. 72.

11. *Lev Ivra*, p. 91.

12. *Teshuvot Ivra* (*Kitvei haGri"a Henkin*, vol. 2), pp. 199–206. In the introduction to his *derashah*, R. Henkin, seeking a position, gave a discourse on the types of discourses rabbis give when seeking a position.

13. R. Yechezkel Abramsky preceeded him in this position.

14. See *Teshuvot Ivra*, pp. 50–2, 180–96.

15. The synagogue is still in existence.

16. Eliyahu Yosef is the name he used in Europe in correspondence, in his notebook, and in his official stamp. The first known use of "Yosef Eliyahu" is found in his Russian passport from 1922. Perhaps a careless passport offi-

cial reversed the name; the mistake was subsequently copied by U.S. immigration authorities and became permanent.

17. R. Epstein returned to Europe, and died in the Minsk ghetto in 1942.

18. Another widely reported account is that R. Henkin kept a notebook in which he recorded any time spent at the office answering halachic questions unrelated to Ezras Torah. He made sure to pay back the time spent.

19. From language in his will.

20. *Eidut leYisrael*, pp. 149–72. Among the many topics discussed are methods of teaching in *yeshivot* and of teaching Hebrew, Hebrew pronunciation, hygiene in synagogue practices, and common mistakes in prayers.

21. BT *Berachot* 31a.

22. *Contra* the canard in the anecdotal *Vintage Wein*, p. 222–4, R. Henkin did not suffer from a debilitating disease at the end of his life. Other glaring mistakes in the chapter about R. Henkin are the claims that he did not publicize his ruling concerning not eating before *teki'ot*, see below, note 24, and that he deferred to R. Moshe Feinstein *z"l* on the question of whether or not Reform marriages require a *get*, see *Kitvei haGri"a Henkin*, vol. 2, pp. 123–5; *Bnei Banim*, II, pp. 145–6. R. Henkin was the major *posek* in America during the 1940s and 1950s; the first volume of R. Feinstein's Resp. *Igrot Moshe* appeared only in 1959 and R. Feinstein became widely accepted in the course of the 1960s, when R. Henkin was in his ninth decade.

23. In 1972 the Ashkenazic Chief Rabbi of Israel, Rabbi Shlomo Goren, issued a controversial ruling concerning the personal status of two brothers. R. Henkin refused to comment on the lengthy halachic arguments, as he was

unable to read them. He did say 1) the Chief Rabbi was a recognized scholar and his ruling in the case at hand could not be summarily dismissed, but 2) for his halachic reasonings to become part of accepted Halacha other authorities must agree with them.

Other rabbis, including great scholars, visited R. Henkin to try to extract a more partisan statement, but he refused. The Israeli newspaper *HaTzofeh*, representing one of the opposing sides, reported only the first half of R. Henkin's statement, while *HaModia*, representing the other, reported only the second half.

24. See *Teshuvot Ivra*, pp. 45–6; Resp. *Bnei Banim*, I, pp. 53–6. R. Henkin also publicized the *issur* of eating before *teki'ot* in the annual Ezras Torah synagogue calendar, where it appears to this day.

25. See *Eidut leYisrael*, p. 161; *Teshuvot Ivra*, p. 6.

26. R. Yaakov Kaminetzky, *z"l*.

27. However, Halacha stipulates a sky-blue strand on each corner.

28. See *Encyclopaedia Judaica Yearbook*, 1974, p. 415. There is a serious error in the *Encyclopaedia Judaica*, vol. 8, *s. v.* Henkin, Joseph Elijah, which states: "His published responsa appear in Chaim Bloch's *Even mi-Kir Tizak* (1953) and his own *Peirushei Lev Ivra* (c. 1925)." *Even mi-Kir Tizak* does not contain any of R. Henkin's responsa but is instead a defamatory pamphlet, heretofore obscure, penned by Bloch against him and the Agudas Harabbonim out of disgruntlement over having lost a *din Torah* heard before R. Henkin and another rabbi.

The source for the confusion is probably the card catalogue of the Jewish Reading Room of the 42nd Street Library in New York, which sub-listed Bloch's pamphlet under "Henkin, Joseph Elijah"; the *Encyclopaedia Ju-*

daica researcher apparently copied the listing without bothering to look up the work. The mistake was repeated twenty years later in the Israeli religious *Encyclopedia Lebeit Yisrael*, which presumably copied it from the *Encyclopaedia Judaica*. I have been told that a future update of the CD-ROM Edition of the *Encyclopaedia Judaica* will correct the error. (For an unrelated but similar lapse in scholarship in the *Encyclopedia Talmudit*, see *Bnei Banim* II, p. 30.).

R. Henkin's published books are: 1) *Peirushei Ivra* (1925), 192 pages. 2) *Mador haHalacha: Ikarei Dinim uMinhagei Beit haKnesset* in *Eidut Leyisrael* (1946), 112 pages. 3) (*Peirushei*) *Lev Ivra* (1956), 176 pages. All these were reprinted in 1981 as *Kitvei haGri"a Henkin*, vol. 1. 4) *Teshuvot Ivra* (*Kitvei haGri"a Henkin*, vol. 2) (1989), 278 pages, edited by my father, Dr. A. Hillel Henkin, *z"l*.

29. See *Avot deRabi Natan*, 14:3.

30. BT *Sanhedrin* 28b.

31. BT *Shabbat* 147b. "This month is for you..." was the first commandment given to Israel; the implication of the mistake was that R. Eleazar ben Arach had abandoned practical Halacha.

32. *Shulchan Aruch, Choshen Mishpat* 268:2. Four cubits in the innermost rooms of a private domain are not "of [practical] Halacha," in the sense that they do not effect a *kinyan*, a halachically valid acquisition of an object. They are not halachic even in a metaphorical sense, for a *posek* must know what is going on in the outside world in order to rule on it. The Talmudic statement "Since the Temple was destroyed, G-d has in His world only the four cubits of Halacha" (*Berachot* 8b) is best understood, not as referring to cloistered Torah study but in a legal sense: G-d owns His world, as it were, through the halachic *kinyan* of

whatever is in His immediate four cubits, since the whole world is His footstool.

33. *Teshuvot Ivra*, pp. 207–210, 215–7.

34. This is supported by G-d's statement to Noah, "...for I have seen you righteous before Me in this generation" (*Bereishit* 7:1). Here "wholesome" is not mentioned, as the verse refers only to the generation of the Flood.

35. This interpretation has also been cited in the name of R. Yosef Kara. Support by *gematria* was subsequently brought by Rabbi Scheinfeld *z"l*, a member of R. Henkin's *minyan*: *bedorotav*, "in his generations," is numerically equivalent (622=622) to *bedor hamabul vedor hapelagah*, "in the generation of the Flood and the generation of the tower of Bavel."

36. BT *Sanhedrin* 108a.

GLOSSARY

admo"r — honorific title of Chassidic rabbis.

aggadah — non-legal part of rabbinical teachings.

agunot — women whose husbands have disappeared and are unable to marry.

a"h — *alav/aleha hashalom*, peace be on him/her.

al kiddush haShem — as a martyr.

amora — a rabbi of the gemara. pl. **amoraim**.

areivut — responsibility for one another.

baal tefillah — prayer leader.

Bamidbar — Numbers.

bar/bat mitzvah — religious coming of age for a boy/girl.

bayit sheni — the Second Temple.

bedi'eved — after the fact.

bein hameitzarim — three-week period of semi-mourning ending with **tishah be'Av**, the fast of the 9th of *Av*.

beit din — rabbinical court.

beit hamikdash — the Temple.

beit midrash — study hall.

ben / bar — son of.

ben Torah — a scholarly, religious person.

Bereishit — Genesis.

birkat hagomel — blessing recited after being saved from danger.

birkat hamazon — grace after meals.

chalitzah — procedure for freeing a childless widow from marrying the late husband's brother.

chacham —religious leader; lit. "wise person."

chametz — leaven.

chaza"l — sages of the Talmud and Midrash.

chazan — cantor, pl. **chazanim**.

Chazon Ish — name used for a recent sage, R. Y. Karelitz, originally the title of his books.

cherem — consecration. Also: excommunication.

chessed — [acts of] mercy, lovingkindness. Alternatively: **gemilut chassadim**.

chiddush — novellum.

chilul haShem — profanation of the Name. **mechalelei haShem** — those who profane the Name.

chumra — optional strictness.

churban — destruction (of the Temple).

daven — (Yiddish) pray.

derashah — homily. pl. **drashot**.

Devarim — Deuteronomy.

din — law; justice. **dinei Torah** — religious court cases.

divrei Torah — words of the Torah; Torah study.

Eichah — Lamentations.

eiruvin — enclosures permitting carrying on the Sabbath.

eit la'asot laShem — religious emergency; lit. "time to act for G-d."

Eretz Yisrael — land of Israel.

erev — evening.

ezrat nashim — women's gallery in a synagogue.

ga'al Yisrael — blessing which immediately precedes the silent morning prayer.

gabbai — sexton.

gadol — great scholar. pl. **gedolim**.

gaon — rabbinical genius; great scholar. pl. **gaonim**. Originally the title of the heads of the Babylonian academies.

gadol hador — preeminent scholar of a generation. pl. **gedolei hador**.

gematria — method of equating words and phrases by assigning numerical values to letters.

get — divorce certificate. pl. **gittin**.

gezar din — verdict.

gezeirah shavah — equivalance (in language). One of the principles of Biblical hermeneutics.

gezeirot — preventive legislation.

haGri"a(h) — *haGaon Rabbi Yosef Eiyahu* (*Henkin*).

Halacha — Jewish religious law. pl. **halachot**.

Halacha lema'aseh — Halacha to be implemented in practice.

haShem — the (Divine) Name; the Tetragrammaton.

hashkafah — outlook; viewpoint.

haskamot — approbations.

hefsek — interruption.

hester panim — G-d's hiding His face.

hirhur — forbidden thoughts.

hora'ah — halachic rulings.

issur — prohibition. **issur veheter** — laws of what is forbidden and permitted.

kabbalat mitzvot — commitment to observe the commandments.

kaddish derabbanan — kaddish recited after Torah study.

kaddish yatom — mourner's kaddish, pl. **kaddishim**.

kavanah — concentration; intent.

kashrut — state of being kosher (halachically permitted for consumption).

kinyan — act of acquiring ownership.

klal Yisrael — entire people of Israel.

kol ishah, kol be'ishah — woman's voice.

lashon hara — talebearing; slander.
lechatchilah — *ab initio*.
lehavdil — term used to distinguish the sacred from the profane; *mutatis mutandis*.

ma'amar — article.
Mashiach — the Messiah.
midah keneged midah — measure for measure.
mide'oraita — stemming from Torah law.
miderabbanan — from rabbinical enactment.
mechitzah — partition between men's and women's galleries.
midrashei hage'ulah — midrashim dealing with the Redemption.
megillah — scroll of Esther. **kri'at megillah**, **mikra megillah** — *megillah* reading.
minhag — custom. pl. **minhagim**.
minyan — prayer quorum. pl. **minyanim**.
midot — ethical standards.
mishnayot — statements of the Mishna.
mitzvah — commandment. pl. **mitzvot**.
moreh — instructor; teacher.
moser — informer.
motza'ei Shabbat — Saturday night.
muktzah — items forbidden to be moved on Sabbaths and holidays.
musaf — additional prayer on Sabbaths and holidays.

na'arah — unmarried girl. pl. **na'arot**.
netzach Yisrael — G-d; lit. "the Eternal of Israel."
nosei keilim — commentators; lit. "armor-bearers."

parshah — chapter.
pesach — Passover holiday
peshat — simple meaning of a text, as opposed to **derash**, homiletics.

pikuach nefesh — saving life.

posek — halachic authority. pl. **poskim**.

posek hador — most eminent *posek* of a generation.

psak — halachic ruling.

puk chazi mai ama davar — see what people do; follow community practice.

rabbeinu — our master (honorific title).

rasha — wicked person, sinner.

rav — rabbi.

rishonim and **achronim** — early and late post-Talmudic rabbinical authorities. The dividing date is c. 1450.

rodef — "pursuer." pl. **rodfim**.

rosh metivta — instructor in a secondary school-level yeshiva.

safek — doubt.

se'ar be'ishah — woman's hair.

seder — Passover evening meal and ritual.

seder Moed — second of six orders of the Mishna and Talmud, dealing primarily with Sabbaths and holidays.

seder Nashim — third order of the Mishna and Talmud, dealing primarily with laws of personal status.

semichah — rabbinical ordination.

Shabbat — the Sabbath.

shaliach tzibur — prayer leader.

Shechinah — Divine presence.

she'elot uteshuvot — collection of responsa.

shehechiyanu — blessing on having lived to reach an important time.

shemittah — sabbatical year.

Shemot — Exodus.

sheva berachot — blessings at a wedding or wedding feast.

shivat Tzion — return to Zion after the Babylonian exile.

shiur — lesson, lecture.
Shulchan Aruch — code of Jewish law.
 Orach Chayim — section dealing with prayers,
 Sabbaths, and holidays. **Yoreh De'ah** — section dealing
 with *kashrut*, menstrual separation, and other laws.
 Even haEzer — section dealing with family laws.
 Choshen Mishpat — section dealing with courts and
 monetary laws.
sugya — Talmudic discussion.

talmidei chachamim — advanced students; scholars.
Tanach — the twenty-four books of the Bible.
tanaim — rabbis of the Mishna.
teki'ot — shofar blowing.
teshuvah — repentantance; also: responsum. pl. **teshuvot**.
tevilah — ritual immersion.
tocheichah — rebuke; Biblical litany of punishments for
 straying from G-d.
treifot — [laws concerning] non-kosher animals and meat.
tzaddik — outstandingly righteous person.
tzitzit — ritual fringes.

va'ad harabbonim — local rabbinical council.
Vayikra — Leviticus.
vorts — (Yiddish) pre-wedding gatherings; lit. "words."

yeihareg ve'al ya'avor — submit to death rather than
 violate.
yeitzer hara — evil inclination.
yirat shamayim — fear of Heaven.
Yom Ha'atzma'ut — Israel Independence Day.

zechut — benefit; merit.
zeicher tzaddik livrachah — may the memory of the
 tzaddik serve as a blessing.
zemirot — hymns at the Sabbath table.

zimun — responsive invitation to take part in *birkat hamazon*.

z"l — *zichrono/zichronah liverachah*, may his/her memory serve as a blessing.